CLARKSON POTTER/PUBLISHERS
NEW YORK

# MasterChef

## JUNIOR

## COOKBOOK

Bold Recipes and Essential Techniques
to Inspire Young Cooks

foreword by

*christina tosi*

Published in the United States by Clarkson Potter/
Publishers, an imprint of the Crown Publishing
Group, a division of Penguin Random House LLC,
New York.
crownpublishing.com
clarksonpotter.com

CLARKSON POTTER is a trademark and POTTER
with colophon is a registered trademark of Penguin
Random House LLC.

MasterChef Junior is a registered trademark of
Shine Television, LLC, and is used under license.
The MasterChef logo and MasterChef "M-Swirl"
logo are registered trademarks of Shine Limited
and are used under license. All rights reserved.
MasterChef is based on a format created by Franc
Roddam in association with Ziji Productions.

FOX™ Fox and its related entities. All rights
reserved.

Library of Congress Cataloging-in-Publication Data.
Names: McLachlan, Clay, photographer.
Title: MasterChef Junior cookbook: bold recipes
    and essential techniques to inspire young
    cooks/MasterChef Junior; photographs by Clay
    McLachlan.
Other titles: MasterChef Junior.
Description: First edition. | New York: Clarkson
    Potter/Publishers, [2017] | Includes index.
Identifiers: LCCN 2016056230 | ISBN
    9780451499127 (trade pbk. w/flaps) |
    ISBN 9780451499134 (eISBN)
Subjects: LCSH: Cooking. | LCGFT: Cookbooks.
Classification: LCC TX714.M3756 2017 |
    DDC 641.5—dc23 LC record available at
    https://lccn.loc.gov/2016056230

ISBN 978-0-451-49912-7
Ebook ISBN 978-0-451-49913-4

Printed in China

Book and cover design by Ian Dingman
Cover photographs by Evan Sung

10  9  8  7  6  5  4  3  2

First Edition

# CONTENTS

# foreword

Yes. Yes. The hype is real. These home cooks, ages eight to thirteen years old, are *that good* in the kitchen. Cooking—the art, the appeal of spending time in the kitchen—has become a cultural phenomenon, and instead of taking piano lessons, learning karate, or going to ballet classes, kids are learning to cook. Information is at their fingertips, from online how-to videos, to elementary and middle school after-school cooking classes, to enthralling cooking shows on TV (cough-*MasterChef*-cough), to private tutors, to the very art of dining at a nice restaurant. Kids are picking up the tools and techniques needed to become great chefs at an early age. Yes, this means if you're a parent, you can start demanding home-cooked meals much earlier than you had planned, and make it one of their chores. But the most exciting part for me is seeing the way young chefs' minds work. They're much too young to fear failure, they're still learning the rules of the road, and their imaginations run wild every single day. So the food they create, the flavor combinations they discover, the macaron recipes they bake up in the oven—they're like nothing you've ever had, seen, or whipped up before.

As a judge on *MasterChef Junior,* I get to spend lots of time mentoring these kids, and it is a whirlwind. Their minds are sponges. What they don't know now, they learn and form an opinion in about ten minutes. Their sense of wonder, of discovery with ingredients and techniques, is insane. They know no bounds, no limits, so of course they push boundaries and discover things we adults never thought possible. They don't miss a beat. For as much as we teach them, I'm convinced they're there to school us, too.

These young home cooks are raising the bar of home cooking to a whole new level, and I couldn't be more excited. Time in the kitchen is serious, and cooking is a true craft, and the *MasterChef Junior* contestants show us that having a good time and remembering to celebrate the things you create are very important. They are an incredible breed of poised but fun-loving chefs who constantly remind me to try new things, to celebrate mistakes made in the kitchen, and to take it all in stride. To go big and have fun doing it.

Who are these kids? Where in the world did they come from? Though they're probably a few years shy of opening their own restaurants, bakeries, food trucks, and culinary schools, *they* are the future of food, and I'm excited that this book shares their amazing food with all of you.

*christina tosi*

# INTRODUCTION

Kids are cooking like never before. There's a fascination with food these days that has caught on with all generations, and young home cooks are more curious than ever to get into the thick of it. *MasterChef Junior* has emerged as a beloved source of inspiration, entertainment, and encouragement to be bold in the kitchen. A special kids-only zone, this competition TV show gives talented young cooks a place to shine—and test their mettle against their peers. And while the challenges are tough, the friendships that develop are stronger, as the contestants root for one another and share their love of food.

The *MasterChef Junior* kitchen is a unique place where contestants learn to trust themselves, help one another, and have a lot of fun. From Mystery Box Challenges to egg frying tutorials and great instruction from the judges, the kitchen is an incubator where ideas and skills can flourish. And what the contestants do in this space is truly amazing. The dishes they create are so masterfully crafted that the judges often say they could be on fine-dining menus. Would you ever imagine that your Seared Scallops with Jalapeño-Poblano Salsa entrée (page 75) was cooked by a twelve-year-old? Pretty impressive! But as elevated as the cooking is, the kitchen is nonetheless a place for pranks and goofy moments. Like when, in Season 2, Sean expertly cooked nineteen pancakes in six minutes, and then still poured gallons of syrup

on Joe Bastianich's head, even though he didn't have to because he won! Or the time in Season 4 when the junior home cooks retrieved their aprons from a giant piñata that looked like Gordon. Wherever there's food, there's *fun*, and the contestants find new, delicious ways to express themselves daily.

The *MasterChef Junior Cookbook* aims to get more young home cooks into the kitchen by providing excellent recipes and how-to information for honing your cooking skills. It's both a practical tool that really anyone can use to try new techniques and types of dishes in their own home, as well as a celebration of the show. The 100 recipes are inspired by dishes that contestants created in the first five seasons, and there are photos throughout that highlight some of the cool things that happened as the competitors cooked their hearts out to win the title of MasterChef Junior. Scattered throughout are sidebars with tips that both parents and children can use to master some of the handiest skills and techniques, including four ways to prepare fish perfectly (page 72), how to master cooking steak without a grill (page 106), and the secrets to a flawless soufflé (page 228).

Inside, you'll find recipes conveniently organized by type of dish and divided into six chapters: Snacks & Starters, Fish & Shellfish, Meat & Poultry, Pasta, Sides & Salads, and Desserts. We've broken apart some of the more complicated dishes, sorting the different pieces into their appropriate chapters, so that everything is more approachable. For instance, in Season 4, the Red Team faced the challenge of catering a three-Michelin-star-quality lunch for luminaries of the food world. Their final dish was just one plate, but the contents read like a multicourse menu! With roasted venison tenderloin, braised cabbage, creamy parsnip purée, sautéed chanterelle mushrooms, and homemade gnocchi, there was no shortage of creativity in this meal. For simplicity in this book, though, you'll find the recipe for Venison Tenderloin with Braised Cabbage and Parsnip Purée on page 127, and the recipe for homemade gnocchi on page 133. You can easily cook each recipe separately, or you can make it all to replicate what was on the show. We encourage you to mix and match all of the various mains and sides to create something all-together new!

If there is one overarching lesson we've learned from the extraordinary children who have been part of *MasterChef Junior,* it is this: Be creative and imaginative in the kitchen! Don't be afraid to combine ingredients you've never seen together. Draw inspiration from your own culinary background and traditions all over the world. Boldly mix different flavors and techniques, try putting your own twist on a classic dish, something elevated that nods to the simple. You never know what delicious foods may come from innovation. We hope this cookbook inspires you to wear your aprons proudly and keep cooking!

# SNACKS & STARTERS

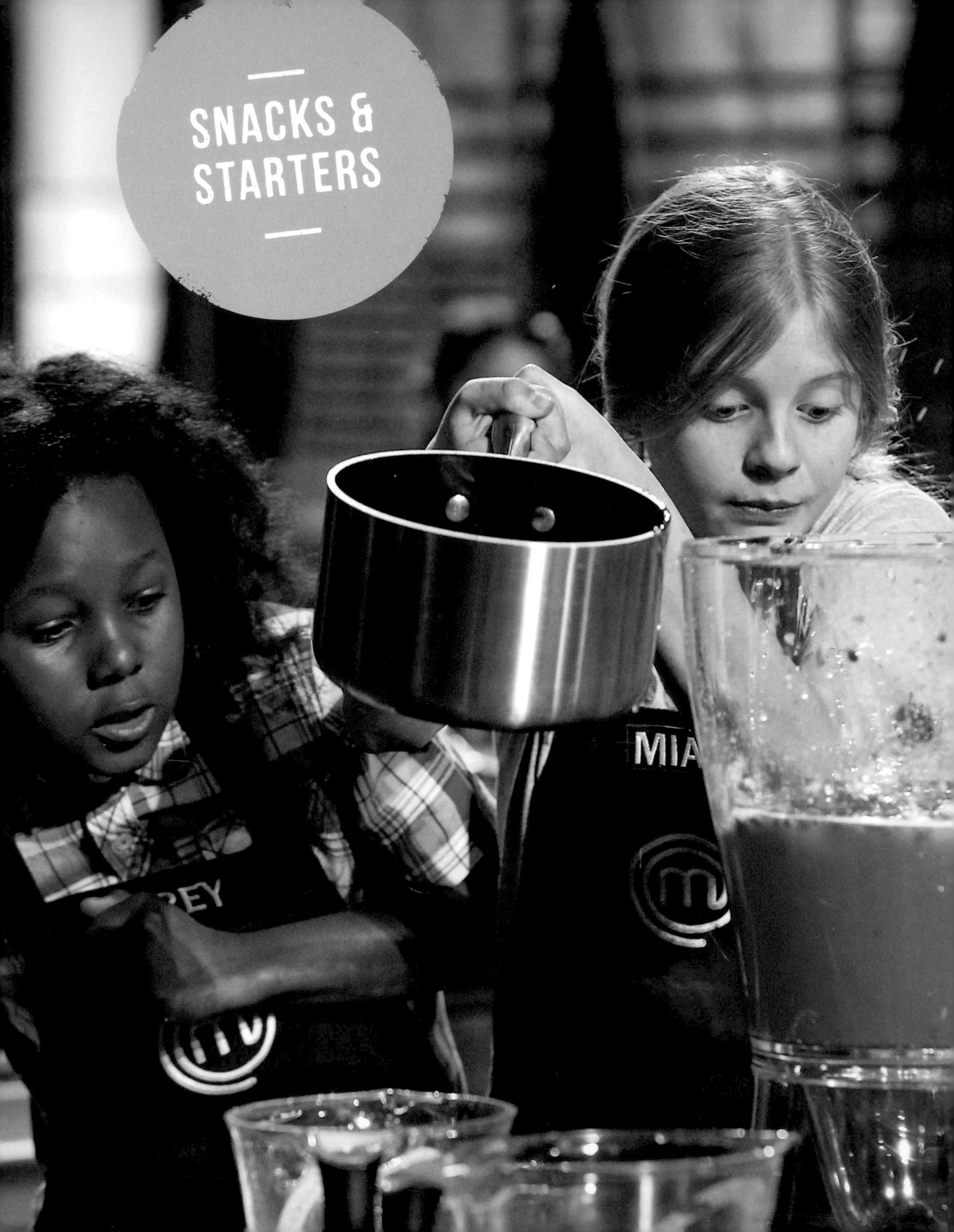

These fritters and romesco sauce are delicious together, but if you want to serve it exactly as Jasmine did, whip up the Green Papaya and Bell Pepper Salad (page 177) and arrange a small handful of it on top of the fritters. You'll notice there's a pepper theme running through this dish, giving it a complex, slightly spicy flavor. Building meals around a single flavor is a great way to create an unexpected but coordinated dish. Pick your favorite vegetable and see where it takes you!

# SCALLOP AND SMOKED TROUT FRITTERS

## with ROMESCO SAUCE  *serves 4*

**Romesco Sauce**
¾ teaspoon ground cinnamon
1 tablespoon dark chile powder
½ tablespoon ground allspice
1 teaspoon ground cloves
¾ teaspoon cayenne
1 tablespoon red curry powder
½ cup roasted salted peanuts
4 ounces roasted piquillo peppers
1 cup roasted red bell peppers
1 tablespoon sherry vinegar
1 tablespoon olive oil
Kosher salt

**Scallop and Smoked Trout Fritters**
Vegetable oil, for frying
2 cups bay scallops, cut into quarters
1 cup chopped smoked trout
1 red bell pepper, finely chopped
2 teaspoons minced garlic
2 tablespoons chopped fresh chives
Zest of 2 key limes
2 large egg yolks
2 tablespoons mayonnaise

2 tablespoons all-purpose flour
2 cups plus 2 tablespoons panko bread crumbs
4 roasted piquillo peppers, finely chopped
Kosher salt

Small bunch of micro cilantro, for garnish

**1.** Make the romesco sauce: In a small bowl, mix together the cinnamon, chile powder, allspice, cloves, cayenne, and red curry powder. Measure 1 tablespoon of this seasoning mixture into a food processor. (There will be leftover seasoning mixture; try it sprinkled over a fillet of snapper or as a dry rub for steak.) Add the peanuts, piquillo peppers, roasted red bell peppers, vinegar, and olive oil. Process until smooth. Season with salt.

**2.** Make the scallop and smoked trout fritters: Pour at least 3 inches of vegetable oil into a heavy-bottomed pot. Heat over medium-high heat to 350°F.

**3.** In a large bowl, combine the scallops, trout, red bell pepper, garlic, chives, lime zest, egg yolks, mayonnaise, flour, 2 tablespoons of the bread crumbs, the piquillo peppers, and a pinch of salt. Put the remaining 2 cups bread crumbs in a shallow

*(Continued)*

bowl. Using your hands, shape the scallop mixture into 12 balls about 1 inch in diameter and roll them in the remaining 2 cups bread crumbs.

**4.** When the oil is ready, working in batches, carefully fry the fritters until golden brown and crisp, about 3 minutes per batch. To check for doneness, you can cut open a fritter to make sure the middle is cooked through and no longer doughy. Transfer to a wire rack or a plate lined with paper towels and let cool slightly.

**5.** To serve, pile the fritters on a large platter. Serve the romesco sauce on the side for dipping. Garnish with a few sprigs of micro cilantro.

## ELEVATING FINGER FOOD FOR THE FINALE

For her Season 5 finale, Jasmine chose to elevate the seafood fritter (a classic finger food) to a restaurant-quality dish. "I wanted to do something simple," she says, "but with flavors that would impress the judges. Also, I wanted to do a dish in honor of my father's Jamaican heritage." With that in mind, she combined scallops and smoked trout here, rather than the other types of seafood more commonly found in fritters, like crab or cod. "I hoped these flavors would be more appealing to the judges and make the dish more sophisticated," Jasmine says. She also served the fritters with a peppery romesco sauce and Green Papaya and Bell Pepper Salad (page 177), both of which added to the sophistication and overall complexity of the dish.

So how can home cooks elevate other classic foods? Jasmine suggests three ways to take a dish to the next level: "First, remember your audience and you will understand what they like and will find fancier alternatives that they will enjoy. Second, take a classic idea and a chef's idea, and then find somewhere in between those two with your cooking. Third, keep it simple and make sure you have the basics down." Above all else, she believes we should "never be afraid to try an old dish in a new way!"

These Baltimore-style crab cakes are well seasoned and, in true Maryland style, don't have a lot of filler ingredients—just enough mayonnaise and egg to hold them together. True Baltimore crab cakes would be made from the small, sweet Chesapeake Bay blue crabs this region is famous for, but you could use whatever your fishmonger has available. Instead of making eight small crab cakes to serve four people, try shaping them into even smaller, bite-size cakes for a delicious passed appetizer.

CONTESTANT:
Jack
—
SEASON 1

# CRAB CAKES
## with GARLIC AIOLI  serves 4

1 pound lump crabmeat

1 large egg yolk

½ cup panko bread crumbs

1½ teaspoons Worcestershire sauce

1 teaspoon Old Bay seasoning

½ teaspoon minced fresh thyme leaves

1 cup plus 2 tablespoons mayonnaise

2 garlic cloves, minced

½ cup sour cream

1 tablespoon celery seeds

Finely grated zest and juice of 1 lemon

¼ cup extra-virgin olive oil

2 tablespoons finely chopped fresh chives

Kosher salt and freshly ground black pepper

Vegetable oil

8 butter lettuce leaves, for serving

Lemon wedges, for garnish

**1.** Preheat the oven to 300°F.

**2.** In a large bowl, mix together the crabmeat, egg yolk, bread crumbs, Worcestershire sauce, Old Bay seasoning, thyme, and 2 tablespoons of the mayonnaise until well blended. Using your hands, gently form the mixture into 8 patties that are about 1 inch thick. Refrigerate for 10 to 15 minutes.

**3.** Meanwhile, make the garlic aioli by mixing together the remaining 1 cup mayonnaise, the garlic, sour cream, celery seeds, lemon zest, lemon juice, olive oil, and chives. Season with salt and pepper.

**4.** Heat a large pan over medium-high heat and add enough vegetable oil to coat the bottom of the pan. Add as many crab cakes to the pan as will fit in a single layer. Sear until golden brown on the first side, then flip and sear on the second side until golden brown, 3 to 4 minutes per side. Transfer to a wire rack set over a rimmed baking sheet and keep warm in the oven while you cook the remaining crab cakes.

**5.** To serve, spoon some garlic aioli in the center of each plate and place 2 leaves of butter lettuce to the side. Place 2 crab cakes between the lettuce and garlic aioli. Garnish with lemon wedges and serve.

Dara's inventive appetizer unites two equally delicious ways to prepare fresh ahi tuna. One is a raw, *poke*-style salad of marinated cubes of the fish. The other is a whole block of it, quickly seared in a hot pan, then sliced and served with radish and sea bean.

CONTESTANT:
Dara
—
SEASON 1

# DUO OF AHI TUNA

serves 2

1 (3-ounce) block ahi (yellowfin) tuna, plus 2 ounces ahi (yellowfin) tuna, cut into ½-inch cubes

3 tablespoons soy sauce

1¼ teaspoons finely grated fresh ginger

1 teaspoon minced garlic

1 cup steamed white rice

1 teaspoon rice vinegar

Kosher salt

1 teaspoon thinly sliced scallion

¼ teaspoon black sesame seeds

1 tablespoon toasted sesame oil

6 (1-inch-long) pieces of sea bean (see Tip)

1 radish, thinly sliced

**1.** Combine the block of ahi tuna, 2 tablespoons of the soy sauce, 1 teaspoon of the ginger, and the garlic in a small dish and let marinate while you prepare the rest of the dish.

**2.** Season the cooked rice with the vinegar and a pinch of salt. Form into a patty and set aside.

**3.** In a small bowl, combine the diced ahi tuna, scallion, sesame seeds, remaining 1 tablespoon soy sauce, and remaining ¼ teaspoon ginger. Let marinate while you sear the block of ahi tuna.

**4.** In a small nonstick sauté pan, heat the sesame oil over medium-high heat. Sear the block of ahi tuna, turning to equally cook on all sides, for about 45 seconds total. Remove the fish from the pan and let rest. Add the rice patty to the pan and sear, turning to cook both sides, about 1 minute total.

**5.** Cut the seared tuna into 3 slices and arrange them on one side of a plate, and then scatter the sea bean and radish around the slices. Place the rice patty on the other side of the plate and pile the diced tuna on top. Serve.

TIP Sea bean, sometimes called sea asparagus, is a salty, crisp, and bright green plant that is most often found near the ocean. They're in season during the summer, so if you live near the coast or a salty marsh, look for sea beans at your local farmer's market. You can also order them online, or substitute with green beans or asparagus for a nice crunch.

In this dish, Alexander combines many different textures—the crisp edges of toasted olive bread, the smoothness of roasted red pepper purée, and the pop of fresh cherry tomatoes—while also bringing together several robust flavors flawlessly. Judge Joe Bastianich said he loved this dish because "you can taste every individual component as you eat it," and judge Graham Elliot thought the presentation was beautiful and very natural, as if "you stumbled upon it in the woods." We bet this is the first time you've ever found shrimp in the forest, but after trying these crostini, you may end up looking for them the next time you take a walk!

# CROSTINI WITH SHRIMP,

**ROASTED RED PEPPER, and PINE NUT PURÉE**   serves 4 to 6

1 loaf olive bread, sliced

Extra-virgin olive oil

Kosher salt

2 garlic cloves

Freshly ground black pepper

6 large shrimp, peeled, deveined, and sliced in half lengthwise

½ cup roasted red peppers

2 tablespoons kalamata olives, pitted

1 cup toasted pine nuts, plus 2 tablespoons for garnish (see Tip, opposite)

¾ cup mixed color cherry tomatoes, halved

Zest and juice of 2 lemons

¼ teaspoon crushed red pepper flakes

2 tablespoons micro basil, for garnish

**1.** Preheat the oven to 350°F.

**2.** Brush the bread slices with olive oil and sprinkle with salt. Place the bread on a baking sheet and toast in the oven until golden brown and crisp, 10 minutes. As soon as you remove the baking sheet from the oven, rub the garlic cloves across the toast.

**3.** Season the shrimp with salt and black pepper. In a large pan, heat 2 tablespoons olive oil over medium-high heat. Add the shrimp and cook until pink, about 2 minutes.

**4.** In a food processor or blender, combine the roasted red peppers, olives, and 2 tablespoons olive oil and purée until smooth. Transfer to a bowl and season with salt and black pepper.

**5.** In the food processor, purée 1 cup of pine nuts and 2 tablespoons olive oil. Transfer to a bowl and season with salt and pepper.

**6.** In a medium bowl, toss the tomatoes with the lemon zest, lemon juice, red pepper flakes, 2 teaspoons olive oil, and a pinch each of salt and black pepper.

**7.** To assemble the crostini, place a few pieces of toast on each plate. Spoon some of the roasted red pepper purée and the pine nut purée over the toast. Top with the shrimp and tomatoes. Serve garnished with the micro basil and whole pine nuts.

**TIP** To toast any kind of nut, spread a single layer of nuts on a rimmed baking sheet and toast in a preheated 350°F oven until lightly browned and fragrant, 8 to 12 minutes. Alternatively, place the nuts in a small, dry pan on the stovetop and heat over medium-high heat. Stir them regularly and keep a close eye on the pan, because once they start toasting, nuts can burn quickly!

"Don't be afraid
to be adventurous
and try new things!"
—Addison

Addison's stunning season finale appetizer combines several Japanese-inspired elements that repeat across the dish. For example, the spot prawns marinate in a sesame oil dressing and the seaweed salad has both black and white sesame seeds, echoing that toasty, nutty flavor throughout the dish. Try choosing a specific cuisine and identifying some of its core flavors. Then weave these into your favorite dish to create something altogether new!

# SPOT PRAWNS WITH SEAWEED SALAD,
## SOUR PLUMS, and TOGARASHI PUFFED RICE   serves 4

**Spot Prawns**
Kosher salt
12 large Santa Barbara spot prawns
1 garlic clove
1 (1-inch) piece fresh ginger, peeled
1 tablespoon sesame oil
1 cup loosely packed fresh mint
1 cup sliced scallions, white and green parts
1 tablespoon yuzu juice (see page 176)
2 tablespoons fresh lime juice, pluse more as needed
1 cup grapeseed oil
Freshly ground black pepper

**Seaweed Salad**
1 cup fresh seaweed
1 cup sea beans (see Tip, page 19)
4 fresh shiso leaves, thinly sliced
2 tablespoons fresh lime juice, plus more if needed
1 tablespoon white sesame seeds, toasted (see Tip, page 57)
1 tablespoon black sesame seeds, toasted (see Tip, page 57)
Kosher salt

**Sour Plums**
4 sour plums
3 tablespoons honey

**Togarashi Puffed Rice**
1 cup puffed rice
2 tablespoons togarashi seasoning blend (see Tip, page 24)
1 tablespoon grapeseed oil

**1.** Make the spot prawns: Bring a large pot of salted water to a boil. Set a bowl of ice water beside the stove. Cook the spot prawns in the boiling water until opaque, 3 to 4 minutes. Immediately transfer to the ice bath. Peel and devein the prawns.

**2.** In a blender, combine the garlic, ginger, sesame oil, mint, scallions, yuzu juice, lime juice, and grapeseed oil and blend until smooth. Season with salt and pepper. Transfer the marinade to a bowl. Add the prawns and marinate for at least 30 minutes.

*(Continued)*

**3.** Meanwhile, make the seaweed salad: In a medium bowl, combine the seaweed, sea beans, shiso, lime juice, and sesame seeds. Season with more lime juice and salt, if needed.

**4.** Make the sour plums: Cut each sour plum into thin slices, avoiding the pit. Heat the honey in a small pan over medium heat. Add the sour plum slices and cook until caramelized, 3 to 4 minutes.

**5.** Make the togarashi puffed rice: Combine the puffed rice, togarashi, and grapeseed oil in a medium bowl.

**6.** To serve, place the seaweed salad in the center of each of four plates. Top with the spot prawns and sour plums. Sprinkle with togarashi puffed rice.

TIP Togarashi is a Japanese spice blend predominantly made of dried chile peppers and often including dried mandarin orange, sesame seeds, and seaweed flakes. Look for it in Asian grocery stores, and test it out on your favorite dish for a fun, new version!

"I made so many friends on the show. We all had so much fun in the MasterChef kitchen and spending time together when we weren't filming. We all stay in touch and several of us have visited each other since the show ended." —Addison

When Logan presented this colorful dish, judge Gordon Ramsay absolutely loved the bright, luminous color of the saffron aioli. He said that if the aioli could talk, it would probably be saying, "Look at me! I'm here for business." Logan infused the aioli with natural smoky flavors by using a handheld food smoker and a large plastic bag. Don't worry if you don't happen to have a handheld food smoker; the aioli is fantastic as it is.

# GRILLED PRAWNS

## with SMOKED SAFFRON AIOLI and OLIVE-CAPER RELISH  serves 4

½ teaspoon saffron, plus a pinch
1 teaspoon warm water
1 cup mayonnaise
2 garlic cloves, minced
1 tablespoon Dijon mustard
1 teaspoon fresh lemon juice
1¼ cups olive oil, plus more for drizzling

¼ cup capers, drained
¼ cup kalamata olives, pitted
2 teaspoons fresh thyme leaves
2 teaspoons fresh oregano leaves
3 or 4 slices rustic white bread, crusts removed, bread torn into bite-size pieces

12 Santa Barbara spot prawns, heads and shells removed
2 heads baby romaine lettuce, washed and quartered
Kosher salt and freshly ground black pepper

**1.** Combine the pinch of saffron and the warm water in a medium bowl and let soak for 5 minutes. Add the mayonnaise, 1 of the garlic cloves, the mustard, and the lemon juice. Mix well. Place the bowl inside a 1-gallon resealable plastic bag. Load a handheld food smoker with hickory chips and insert the tube of the smoker into the bag. Let the bag fill with smoke while you prepare the rest of the dish.

**2.** In a small saucepan, warm ¼ cup of the olive oil and the remaining ½ teaspoon saffron over low heat for 10 minutes. Remove the pan from the heat and let cool to room temperature.

**3.** In a food processor, combine the remaining garlic clove, the capers, olives, thyme, oregano, and remaining 1 cup olive oil. Pulse until combined but still somewhat chunky.

**4.** Preheat the oven to 350°F.

**5.** Toss the bread with the saffron oil, spread the bread out on a baking sheet, and toast in the oven until golden brown, about 3 minutes.

**6.** Heat a cast-iron grill pan over high heat. Skewer each prawn before grilling to prevent curling. Drizzle the prawns and lettuce with olive oil and season with salt and pepper. Grill the lettuce until charred on one side, about 2 minutes. Grill the skewered prawns, flipping once, until just done on the outside and slightly translucent in the center, about 2 minutes on each side. Remove and discard the skewers.

**7.** To serve, spread about ¼ cup of the smoked saffron aioli across the center of each plate. Spoon about 1 tablespoon of the olive-caper relish over the aioli. Place 2 quarters of grilled lettuce over the relish and top with 3 prawns. Sprinkle a few bread crumbs around each plate.

"In the *MasterChef Junior* kitchen, I learned to set a standard of excellence for myself and understand why food is what we live, love, and share. I sometimes forgot how much I love to cook in all this, but honestly I learned from Chef Ramsay and Chef Elliot to find my own standard and meet it and raise it and meet it again." —Logan

Served whole, these fried fish make quite the impression! But if you really want to make "yucky" ingredients into a "yummy" surprise, pair them with the Brussels Sprout Stir-Fry (page 167) as Sarah did on the show. Look for whole fresh sardines at a well-stocked fish market. If you can't find them, try any other small, full-flavored fish, such as fresh anchovies, smelts, small herring, or baby mackerel. Don't be afraid to try something new just because it seems icky! You never know what might become your new secret weapon.

# FRIED SARDINES

serves 4

Vegetable oil, for frying
1 cup rice flour
1 tablespoon cayenne

1 tablespoon crushed red pepper flakes
1 tablespoon kosher salt

2 teaspoons freshly ground black pepper
12 whole fresh sardines, gutted and scaled

**1.** Pour at least 3 inches of vegetable oil into a heavy-bottomed pot. Heat over medium-high heat to 350°F.

**2.** In a shallow dish, combine the rice flour, cayenne, red pepper flakes, salt, and black pepper. Dredge the sardines in the flour mixture, coating all sides.

**3.** When the oil is ready, carefully fry the sardines until golden brown and crisp, about 4 minutes. Transfer to a wire rack or a plate lined with paper towels and let cool slightly. Serve warm.

This dish has a playful repetition of shapes: perfectly round polenta cakes, golden brown seared scallops, and tiny quail eggs fried sunny-side up. Even the pickled peppers are circles! Not only visually impressive, these scallops are also delicious. The herby chimichurri sauce drizzled over the top brightens and unites the whole plate.

Team Challenge — SEASON 5

# SCALLOPS WITH CHIMICHURRI,
## POLENTA CAKES, and PICKLED PEPPERS    serves 4

### Chimichurri
¼ cup finely chopped fresh flat-leaf parsley
¼ cup finely chopped fresh cilantro
¼ cup finely chopped fresh dill
¼ cup finely chopped fresh tarragon
2 garlic cloves, minced
1 tablespoon finely chopped shallot
½ teaspoon ground Aleppo pepper
1½ cups olive oil
Kosher salt

### Pickled Peppers
1½ cups champagne vinegar
½ cup sugar
½ cup honey
1½ teaspoons coriander seeds
1 cinnamon stick
4 baby orange bell peppers, thinly sliced into rounds
4 baby yellow bell peppers, thinly sliced into rounds
4 baby red bell peppers, thinly sliced into rounds
¼ serrano chile, thinly sliced into rounds
1 cup ice cubes

### Polenta Cakes
2 cups whole milk
2 cups chicken stock
1 bunch fresh basil
1 cup coarsely ground cornmeal
Kosher salt
3 tablespoons grapeseed oil

### Scallops
6 large scallops, halved lengthwise
Kosher salt and freshly ground black pepper
2 tablespoons grapeseed oil, plus more as needed
12 quail eggs

10 sugar snap peas, steamed until tender and sliced on an angle, for garnish
Purple micro radish greens, for garnish

**1.** Make the chimichurri: In a medium bowl, combine the parsley, cilantro, dill, tarragon, garlic, shallot, Aleppo pepper, and olive oil. Season with salt.

**2.** Make the pickled peppers: In a medium saucepan, bring the vinegar, sugar, honey, coriander seeds, and cinnamon stick to a simmer over medium heat, stirring until the sugar has dissolved. Simmer for

*(Continued)*

10 minutes. Strain the liquid through a fine-mesh sieve into a medium bowl and discard the solids. Add the bell peppers and serrano. Add the ice cubes and let the peppers pickle and cool in the liquid for at least 1 hour.

**3.** Make the polenta cakes: In a medium pot, bring the milk and stock to a simmer over medium-high heat. Add the basil, remove the pot from the heat, cover the pot, and let steep for 10 minutes. Remove and discard the basil. Return the pot to the stovetop over low heat and whisk in the cornmeal and a pinch of salt. Cook, stirring often, until creamy and tender, 10 minutes. Transfer the polenta to a 9 by 13-inch baking dish and let cool to room temperature, about 2 hours. Using a 1- to 2-inch circle cutter, cut out at least 12 rounds of the cooled polenta.

**4.** In a large pan, heat the grapeseed oil over medium heat. Add the polenta cakes and cook until golden brown on both sides, about 3 minutes

per side. Transfer the polenta cakes to a plate and season lightly with salt.

**5.** Make the scallops: Season the scallops with salt and pepper on both sides. In a large nonstick pan, heat the grapeseed oil over medium heat. Add the scallops and sear until golden brown, about 1 minute per side. Transfer to a plate. Add more oil to the pan as needed to coat the bottom. Gently break the quail eggs one at a time into the pan, making sure they do not touch. Fry until the whites are cooked through, 1 to 2 minutes. Transfer to the plate with the scallops.

**6.** To serve, arrange 3 polenta cakes and 3 scallop halves in the center of each of four plates. Place a quail egg on top of each polenta cake. Spoon chimichurri over and around the scallops. Garnish with pickled peppers, sugar snap peas, and micro radish.

Dara made these pickled vegetables as an accompaniment for the Glazed Lollipop Wings (page 38), but they would also bring a welcome burst of acidity and brightness to Chicken Liver Pâté with Brûléed Pear and Parsley Salad (page 37), Scallop and Smoked Trout Fritters with Romesco Sauce (page 15), or even Fish Tacos with Guacamole (page 64). It doesn't take much time at all to quick-pickle the vegetables, and once pickled, they will keep for months in the refrigerator. Whip up a batch today and use them to add a tart, crunchy garnish any time a dish needs it!

CONTESTANT:
Dara
—
SEASON 1

# PICKLED VEGETABLES

makes about 1 pint

2 large carrots
1 bunch red radishes

1 English cucumber
1 cup white wine vinegar

1 cup sugar

**1.** Using a mandoline or a very sharp knife, thinly slice the carrots, radishes, and cucumber. Place the vegetables in a medium bowl or jar.

**2.** In a small saucepan, combine the vinegar and sugar. Bring to a boil over medium-high heat and cook, stirring, until the sugar dissolves completely.

**3.** Pour the hot vinegar mixture over the sliced vegetables. Let cool to room temperature before serving.

**4.** Store the vegetables in the pickling liquid in an airtight container in the refrigerator for up to 3 months.

The star of this dish is the homemade herbed ricotta, a creamy cheese that complements the earthy flavor of the roasted beets. You could of course buy ricotta, but the homemade version is quick—it can be done while the beets roast! Plus, the fresh flavor of the homemade version is well worth the effort, and making your own cheese really shows off your skills in the kitchen.

# ROASTED BEETS
## with HERBED RICOTTA serves 4 to 6

4 small Chioggia beets, scrubbed
4 small golden beets, scrubbed
Extra-virgin olive oil
½ lemon
Kosher salt and freshly ground
    black pepper
2 cups whole milk

1 cup buttermilk
3 tablespoons heavy cream, plus
    more as needed
3 tablespoons white wine vinegar
1 tablespoon plus 2 teaspoons
    chopped fresh mint
1 tablespoon plus 2 teaspoons
    chopped fresh chives

1 tablespoon plus 2 teaspoons
    chopped fresh thyme
1½ teaspoons finely grated
    lemon zest
½ cup apricot jam
Pumpernickel bread, thinly sliced
    into 3½ by ½-inch rectangles
Micro basil, for garnish

1. Preheat the oven to 350°F.

2. Place the red beets and yellow beets on two separate pieces of aluminum foil. Drizzle with olive oil. Wrap the foil around the beets. Roast until tender when poked with a fork, about 45 minutes. Unwrap the foil, and let the beets cool. When cool, use your fingers or a clean kitchen towel to rub off the skins and discard. Cut each beet into quarters and place in a bowl. Add a squeeze of lemon juice, season with salt and pepper, and toss to evenly coat.

3. Meanwhile, in a medium saucepan, combine the milk, buttermilk, and cream. Warm the mixture over medium heat until it reaches 175°F, then remove the pan from the heat and gently stir in the vinegar. Let sit for 20 minutes.

4. Transfer the milk mixture to a cheesecloth-lined sieve set over a bowl. Place in the refrigerator and let strain for about 15 minutes. Spoon the strained curds into a medium bowl and fold in 1 tablespoon of the mint, 1 tablespoon of the chives, 1 tablespoon of the thyme, and 1 teaspoon of the lemon zest. The ricotta should have a spreadable consistency. If not, add more cream, 1 tablespoon at a time, folding to incorporate, until it does. Season with salt and pepper.

5. In a small bowl, stir together the apricot jam, the remaining ½ teaspoon lemon zest, and the remaining 2 teaspoons each mint, chives, and thyme.

6. Drizzle olive oil over the pumpernickel. Place the slices on a baking sheet and toast in the oven until crisp, about 5 minutes.

7. To serve, arrange some roasted beets in the center of each plate. Spread about ¼ cup of the herbed ricotta alongside the beets and spoon 1 to 2 tablespoons of the apricot jam mixture over the ricotta. Garnish with micro basil. Serve with the toasted pumpernickel.

For this elegant appetizer, Oona used a kitchen torch to brulée slices of pear. A kitchen torch is an inexpensive, fun tool that can also be put to great use for desserts like the Chocolate Churros with Toasted Marshmallow Whipped Cream (page 233). If you don't have one, you can place the sugared pear slices under a broiler. Just be sure to watch carefully and remove the slices as soon as the sugars caramelize. They will cook quickly, and you don't want to end up with burnt pears!

# CHICKEN LIVER PÂTÉ

## with BRÛLÉED PEAR and PARSLEY SALAD   makes 15 to 20 crostini

2 tablespoons grapeseed oil
½ pound chicken livers, cleaned
4 marinated white anchovies
2 tablespoons chicken stock
Kosher salt and freshly ground
    black pepper

1 baguette
¼ cup extra-virgin olive oil, plus
    more for brushing
2 garlic cloves
1 Anjou pear, cored and thinly
    sliced

2 tablespoons sugar
1 tablespoon fresh lemon juice
1 cup fresh flat-leaf parsley leaves
Flaky sea salt

**1.** In a large sauté pan, heat the grapeseed oil over high heat. Add the chicken livers and anchovies and cook, stirring, until evenly browned, 4 to 5 minutes. Transfer to a food processor. Pour in the stock and process until smooth. Season with kosher salt and pepper.

**2.** Preheat the oven to 375°F.

**3.** Slice the baguette on a slight angle and brush each piece with olive oil. Arrange the slices in a single layer on a baking sheet. Toast in the oven until golden brown and crisp, about 10 minutes. Remove the pan from the oven and immediately rub the garlic on each piece of toast.

**4.** Spread the pear slices out on the same baking sheet. Sprinkle lightly with the sugar. Using a kitchen torch, torch each pear slice until caramelized. While still warm, season with kosher salt.

**5.** In a medium bowl, whisk together the olive oil and the lemon juice. Add the parsley and toss to coat. Season with flaky sea salt.

**6.** To assemble the crostini, spread about 1 tablespoon of chicken liver pâté across each piece of toast. Top with a brûléed pear slice and a few leaves of parsley salad. Serve.

Dara used an impressive technique called frenching to create the fun lollipop shape of these chicken wings. This fancy trick is not too complicated and really makes your final dish look polished. Start by scraping the blade of a small knife down along the chicken bone to clean and expose it. That bone then becomes the lollipop stick, a built-in handle to grasp while eating the delicious glazed chicken meat on the other end. You don't necessarily have to do this step if you don't want to—you can leave the wings whole as they are, and they will still make a delicious, impressive dish!

# GLAZED LOLLIPOP WINGS

serves 4

12 chicken wing drummets
Kosher salt and freshly ground black pepper
Vegetable oil, for frying (about 4 cups)

¾ cup honey
½ cup fresh orange juice
1 (2-inch) piece fresh ginger, peeled and sliced
3 tablespoons tamari or soy sauce

1 teaspoon crushed red pepper flakes
1 stalk lemongrass
1 bunch scallions, green parts only, thinly sliced, for garnish

**1.** Preheat the oven to 350°F.

**2.** Using a small knife, remove the meat from the tops of the chicken wing bones by scraping the blade of the knife down along the bones, creating the look of a lollipop. Pat the wings dry and season with salt and pepper.

**3.** Pour at least 3 inches of vegetable oil into a heavy-bottomed pot. Heat over medium-high heat to 350°F.

**4.** Carefully add about half the wings to the hot oil and fry until golden brown, 5 to 6 minutes. Transfer to a wire rack and let cool slightly. Repeat with the second batch of wings.

**5.** In an oven-safe medium saucepan, combine the honey, orange juice, ginger, tamari, and red pepper flakes. Trim the root end of the lemongrass stalk and cut off the top 2 inches or so. Cut the lemongrass in half lengthwise and peel away and discard any tough, papery layers. Using a rolling pin or a meat mallet, smash the lemongrass to release its flavorful oils. Place the bruised lemongrass in the saucepan, cutting it again, if needed, to fit. Bring to a simmer over medium heat. Add the wings and then carefully transfer the pan to the oven. Cook the wings in the glaze, flipping after 10 minutes, until the glaze thickens and coats the wings, 20 minutes total.

**6.** If the glaze is not syrupy and thick, transfer the wings to a plate and return the pan of glaze to the stovetop. Cook over high heat until the glaze is thick, 1 to 2 minutes. Toss the wings in the glaze and serve hot or warm, garnished with scallions.

Traditional Polish pierogi are often filled with a combination of potato, cheese, and onion. But when Jack made these on the show, he added mushrooms to the filling and served them with a mushroom sauce, layering the mushroom elements for a complex and delicious flavor. Demi-glace is a rich brown sauce made by simmering meaty bones and aromatic vegetables. You can purchase it at butcher shops or upscale supermarkets.

# MUSHROOM-POTATO PIEROGI
## with MUSHROOM SAUCE  makes 8

**Mushroom-Potato Pierogi**
Kosher salt
2 russet potatoes, peeled and
  cut into 1-inch pieces
2 tablespoons vegetable oil
1 cup sliced mushrooms

Freshly ground black pepper
All-purpose flour, for rolling
1 (17-ounce) package puff pastry
1 large egg

**Mushroom Sauce**
2 tablespoons extra-virgin olive oil
1 garlic clove, minced
1 shallot, minced
2 cups sliced mushrooms
1 cup demi-glace
2 tablespoons unsalted butter

**1.** Make the pierogi: Preheat the oven to 400°F. Line a baking sheet with parchment paper.

**2.** Bring a large pot of salted water to a boil. Add the potatoes and cook until tender, about 15 minutes. Drain. Transfer the boiled potatoes to a large bowl. Using a potato masher or large fork, mash the potatoes, leaving them a little chunky.

**3.** In a large pan, heat the vegetable oil over medium-high heat. Add the mushrooms and cook, stirring occasionally, until browned in a few places, about 5 minutes. Stir the cooked mushrooms into the mashed potatoes. Season with salt and pepper.

**4.** On a floured surface, roll out the puff pastry. Use a 3- to 4-inch ring cutter or the rim of a glass to punch out 8 circles. Place 1 tablespoon of the filling in the center of each. Fold in half, pressing the edges to

seal. Using a fork, crimp the edges to create a ½-inch border. Place the filled pierogi on the prepared baking sheet and cover with a clean kitchen towel. Repeat with the remaining pastry and filling.

**5.** In a small bowl, stir together the egg, 1 teaspoon water, and a pinch of salt. Brush the egg wash across the tops of the pierogi. Bake until the pastry is golden brown, about 12 minutes. Let cool slightly.

**6.** Make the mushroom sauce: In a large sauté pan, heat the olive oil over medium heat. Add the garlic, shallot, and mushrooms and cook, stirring, until the shallot is translucent, about 4 minutes. Add the demi-glace and butter and cook until the butter has melted completely.

**7.** Serve the pierogi with the warm mushroom sauce alongside for dipping.

These apple fries may look like regular potato fries, and even have a similar texture, but just one bite and you find their unexpected surprise: a juicy, sweet interior! Frying the apple wedges caramelizes their sugar coating and transforms a humble fruit into an extraordinarily creative snack. Why not change up your traditions next time you crave a burger and partner these apple fries with Italian Burgers with Kalamata Olive Relish (page 115)?

CONTESTANT:
Kya
—
SEASON 4

# APPLE FRIES

serves 4

Vegetable oil, for frying
4 Gala apples, cored and cut into
   wedges

½ cup all-purpose flour
¼ cup sugar

Kosher salt

**1.** Pour at least 2 inches of vegetable oil into a heavy-bottomed pot. Heat the oil over medium-high heat to 350°F.

**2.** In a large bowl, combine the apples, flour, and sugar. Toss to coat the apple wedges completely.

**3.** Carefully add about half the floured apples to the hot oil and fry until golden, about 4 minutes. Using a slotted spoon, transfer the apple fries to a paper towel–lined plate and let cool slightly. Repeat to fry the second batch of floured apples. Lightly season the apple fries with salt and serve warm.

These turnovers are crispy and light, with a slightly savory mango filling inside. For dipping, there's an accompanying sauce, a coconut crème anglaise described by judge Joe Bastianich as "perfection." The dish as a whole is a delicious reminder never to be afraid of combining sweet and savory ingredients.

CONTESTANT:
Kayla
—
SEASON 3

# MANGO TURNOVERS
## with COCONUT CRÈME ANGLAISE  *serves 4 to 6*

**Mango Turnovers**
1 tablespoon unsalted butter
2 cups cubed mango
1 teaspoon lime zest
1 tablespoon fresh lime juice
2 tablespoons honey

1 teaspoon cayenne
1 tablespoon finely chopped fresh
    cilantro
All-purpose flour
1 (10 by 15-inch) sheet puff pastry
1 large egg

**Coconut Crème Anglaise**
1 cup unsweetened coconut milk
½ vanilla bean
2 large egg yolks
3 tablespoons sugar

**1.** Preheat the oven to 350°F. Line a baking sheet with parchment paper.

**2.** Make the mango turnovers: In a medium saucepan, melt the butter over medium-high heat. Add the mango and cook, stirring, until caramelized, 5 minutes. Stir in the lime zest, lime juice, honey, cayenne, and cilantro. Let cool to room temperature.

**3.** Cut the sheet of puff pastry into six 5-inch squares, and then cut each square in half diagonally to create a total of 12 triangles. Spoon about 1 tablespoon of the cooled mango filling into the center of each triangle. Fold each triangle in half, pressing the edges of the puff pastry together and crimping the edges with a fork. Place the turnovers on the prepared baking sheet.

**4.** Crack the egg into a small bowl and beat with a fork. Brush the egg wash across the top of each turnover. Bake until golden brown, 25 to 30 minutes.

**5.** Meanwhile, make the coconut crème anglaise: Pour the coconut milk into a small saucepan set over medium-high heat. Cut the vanilla bean in half lengthwise and use the back of the knife to scrape the tiny black seeds into the pan. Bring the coconut milk to a simmer over medium-low heat, then remove the pan from the heat.

**6.** In a medium bowl, whisk together the eggs yolks and sugar. Temper the egg mixture by whisking in a small ladleful of the hot coconut milk. Return the warmed egg mixture to the saucepan and cook, stirring, over low heat until the sauce thickens and coats the back of a spoon, 4 minutes. Strain through a fine-mesh sieve into a bowl, discard the solids, and let cool.

**7.** Serve the turnovers warm, with the coconut crème anglaise on the side.

These chips may be made from kale, but they are as crispy and salty as your favorite brand! Try them on their own as a snack or alongside the burger (page 115) as a fun and interesting alternative to french fries. You can use regular green kale, red kale, or even dinosaur kale, which is sometimes called lacinato or Tuscan kale. Just a warning: They'll go quick, so be prepared to make more!

# KALE CHIPS

serves 8

Vegetable oil, for frying

2 bunches kale (about 3 pounds)

Kosher salt

**1.** Pour at least 2 inches of oil into a heavy-bottomed pot. Heat the oil over medium-high heat to 350°F.

**2.** Wash the kale and dry thoroughly. Using your hands or a knife, remove the stems. Tear the leaves into large bite-size pieces.

**3.** When the oil is ready, carefully add a small handful of kale leaves. Fry until crisp, about 1 minute. Using a wire skimmer, transfer the kale to a wire rack set over paper towels. While the kale chips are still hot, sprinkle with salt. Repeat with the remaining kale. Serve.

# FISH & SHELLFISH

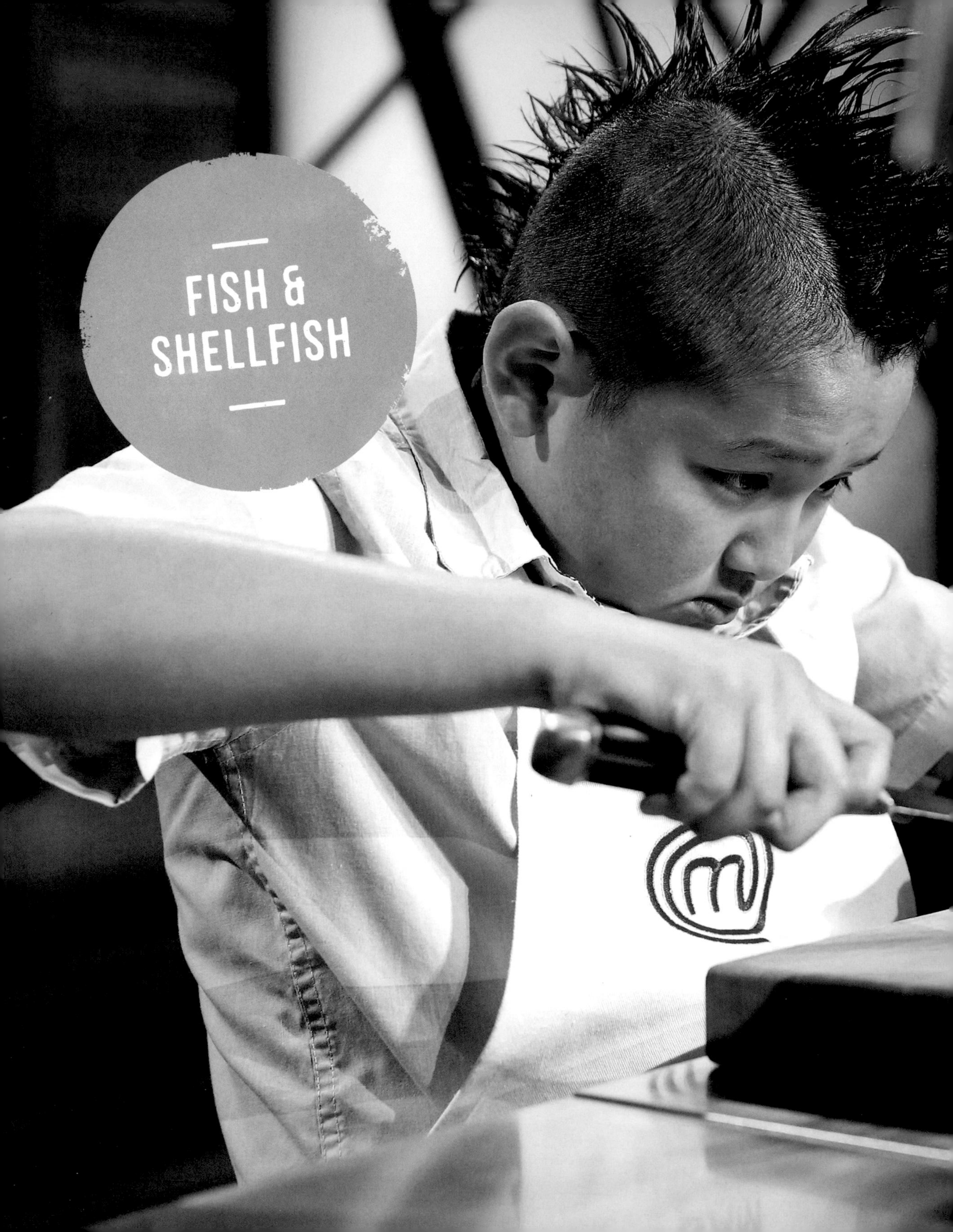

This dish looks beautiful and complicated, but it is even more impressive when you consider how few actual ingredients there are. Abby was able to prepare an elegant main course using essentially only two ingredients: salmon and asparagus. She even transformed the asparagus and the water it was cooked in into a simple yet flavorful sauce! Sometimes a little ingenuity is the key ingredient.

CONTESTANT:
Abby
—
SEASON 2

# SALMON WITH ASPARAGUS, THREE WAYS

serves 4

Kosher salt
48 asparagus stalks, trimmed

5 tablespoons olive oil, plus more for brushing

Freshly ground black pepper
4 (5-ounce) skin-on salmon fillets

**1.** Bring a large pot of salted water to a boil. Add 36 of the asparagus stalks and cook until tender, about 5 minutes. Drain, reserving 1 cup of the cooking liquid. Set 24 of the boiled asparagus stalks aside. Cut the remaining 12 stalks into large pieces and place them in a blender or food processor. Add 2 tablespoons of the olive oil and ½ cup of the reserved cooking liquid and blend until smooth, adding more water if needed to adjust the thickness of the sauce.

**2.** In a large pan, heat 2 tablespoons of the olive oil over high heat. Add the 24 reserved asparagus stalks and cook, turning them occasionally, until beginning to brown, 2 to 3 minutes. Transfer back to the plate and season with salt and pepper.

**3.** Add 1 tablespoon of the olive oil to the pan and reduce the heat to medium. Cut off the bottom part of the remaining 12 uncooked asparagus stalks, leaving only the tips. Add the tips to the pan, season with salt and pepper, and cook, stirring occasionally, until beginning to brown, 2 to 3 minutes. Transfer the tips to the plate with the asparagus spears.

**4.** Preheat the broiler to high.

**5.** Generously brush the salmon with olive oil on both sides and season with salt and pepper. Arrange the fillets skin-side down on a baking sheet and broil until cooked through, 5 to 7 minutes. Carefully remove and discard the salmon skin.

**6.** To serve, divide the whole asparagus spears among four plates, arranging them in the center. Place a salmon fillet on top of the asparagus on each plate and scatter the asparagus tips over and around the salmon. Serve the asparagus sauce on the side.

While the method of cooking this salmon is relatively simple, the other parts of this dish are not. There's a savory coconut sauce that's thick and creamy and a smooth avocado purée. Plus, Jack served Sautéed Broccolini (page 168) and thin slices of mango on the side. All together, these various components make for what the judges called "an artistic, imaginative" dish. You could, of course, choose to serve just the recipe here, but if you really want to impress your guests the way Jack impressed the judges, then gather all the ingredients and get cooking!

CONTESTANT:
Jack
—
SEASON 3

# BROILED SALMON
## with COCONUT SAUCE and AVOCADO PURÉE  serves 4

**Coconut Sauce**
1 (15-ounce) can unsweetened coconut milk
2 tablespoons fresh lime juice
1 shallot, finely chopped
2 tablespoons sugar
2 garlic cloves, finely chopped
1 tablespoon soy sauce
Kosher salt and freshly ground black pepper

**Avocado Purée**
2 ripe avocados, pitted and peeled
2 tablespoons mascarpone cheese
Juice of 1 lemon
2 teaspoons kosher salt

**Salmon**
¼ cup soy sauce
¼ cup fish stock
2 tablespoons honey
4 skin-on salmon fillets, about 4 ounces each
Kosher salt and freshly ground black pepper
4 large Swiss chard leaves, blanched (see Tip, opposite) and stemmed

**1.** Make the coconut sauce: In a small saucepan, combine the coconut milk, lime juice, shallot, sugar, garlic, and soy sauce. Bring to a boil over high heat and cook until reduced by half, 10 to 15 minutes. Season with salt and pepper.

**2.** Make the avocado purée: In a food processor, combine the avocados, mascarpone, lemon juice, and salt. Process until completely smooth.

**3.** Make the salmon: In a small saucepan, combine the soy sauce, fish stock, and honey. Cook over medium heat, stirring, until the honey has dissolved and the sauce thickens slightly, 5 to 7 minutes. Remove the pan from the heat and let cool.

**4.** Preheat the broiler.

**5.** Season the salmon fillets with salt and pepper on both sides. Brush the honey-soy glaze across the salmon and place the fillets skin-side down on a baking sheet. Broil for 5 minutes. Remove from the oven and let cool for about 5 minutes. Once the fillets are cool enough to handle, wrap each fillet with a blanched Swiss chard leaf.

**6.** To serve, spread avocado purée in the bottom of each of four shallow bowls. Set a Swiss chard–wrapped salmon fillet on top of the avocado purée and spoon the coconut sauce around the salmon.

**TIP** Blanching means boiling something briefly, then transferring it to a bowl of ice water to stop the cooking. This method helps to preserve the vibrant color of a vegetable. Swiss chard leaves need to cook for only a few minutes, though other vegetables, like asparagus, need to cook a little longer.

*En croute* refers to wrapping a fillet of fish in puff pastry. Sealed safely inside, the fish stays succulent as it steams in its own juices, while the pastry bakes into a crisp, golden brown crust. Jimmy and Andrew enhanced the flavor of the salmon by "stuffing" it with an herb-flecked butter and grainy mustard. They chose basil and dill, but you can really use any combination of fresh herbs. If you're looking for a side to complement this dish, try the Roasted Potatoes (page 158).

CONTESTANTS:
Jimmy and
Andrew
—
SEASON 3

# SALMON EN CROUTE
## with MINTED PEAS and HOLLANDAISE  serves 4

**Hollandaise**
½ cup white wine vinegar
1 shallot, minced
6 whole black peppercorns
½ cup fresh tarragon leaves
4 large egg yolks
½ cup clarified butter (see Tip, page 54), melted
Kosher salt and freshly ground black pepper

**Minted Peas**
2 tablespoons unsalted butter
3 tablespoons thinly sliced fresh mint
2 cups green peas, blanched (see Tip, page 51)
Kosher salt and freshly ground black pepper

**Salmon en Croute**
⅔ cup unsalted butter, at room temperature
¼ cup finely chopped fresh dill
¼ cup finely chopped fresh basil
2 tablespoons finely grated lemon zest
Kosher salt and freshly ground black pepper
4 skinless salmon fillets, about 4 ounces each
¼ cup whole-grain mustard
All-purpose flour
2 sheets frozen puff pastry, thawed
2 large eggs, beaten

1. Make the hollandaise: In a small saucepan, bring the vinegar, shallot, peppercorns, and tarragon to a simmer over medium-high heat. Cook until reduced by half, 10 to 12 minutes. Strain through a fine-mesh sieve into a bowl and discard the solids.

2. In a medium glass bowl, whisk together the egg yolks and 2 tablespoons of the vinegar reduction. Place the bowl over a pot of simmering water (be sure the bottom of the bowl does not touch the water) and cook over medium-low heat, whisking continuously, until thick and pale in color, 7 to

8 minutes. Slowly drizzle the clarified butter into the egg mixture, whisking until fully incorporated. Season with salt, pepper, and more vinegar reduction.

3. Make the minted peas: In a large sauté pan, melt the butter over medium heat. Add the mint and the blanched peas. Cook, stirring, until the peas are tender, 5 minutes. Season with salt and pepper.

*(Continued)*

**4.** Make the salmon en croute: Preheat the oven to 375°F. Line a baking sheet with parchment paper.

**5.** In a small bowl, combine the butter, dill, basil, lemon zest, and a pinch each of salt and pepper. Slice each salmon fillet in half lengthwise. Spread some of the butter mixture on one half and about 1 tablespoon of mustard on the other half. Stack the halves back on top of each other, with the butter and mustard in the middle. Season each fillet with salt and pepper.

**6.** On a floured work surface, roll out each sheet of puff pastry and cut them in half. Place 1 stacked salmon fillet on each sheet and fold the puff pastry around the salmon, covering it completely but overlapping as little of the pastry as possible. Turn the package over and place seam-side down on the prepared baking sheet. Press down gently to seal the pastry. Using a small knife, score the outside of each

salmon package. Brush with the beaten eggs. Bake until the pastry is golden brown, about 15 minutes. Remove from the oven and let cool for 5 minutes.

**7.** To serve, spoon about ¼ cup of the hollandaise in the center of each of four plates. Place the salmon en croute over the sauce and arrange the minted peas on the side.

TIP Butter is "clarified" when it is cooked until the water evaporates and the milk solids float to the surface. The solids are skimmed, leaving behind perfectly clear butter. In India and other parts of the world, making clarified butter (called ghee) involves cooking the butter long enough to caramelize the milk solids, and even after they are skimmed, their nutty flavor remains. You can buy ghee in Indian grocery stores or online. Regular clarified butter is easy to find online, too.

In the finale episode of Season 2, Samuel poured this curry broth into the serving bowl tableside, which heightened the drama and added to the presentation. Judge Joe Bastianich, recognizing that the fish is from the Arctic and the seasoning inspired by Southeast Asia, said, "I love the idea of taking two opposite parts of the world and putting them on the same plate." All three judges agreed that Samuel had cooked the fish perfectly. "There are chefs in professional kitchens," Gordon Ramsay said, "who overcook this fish time and time again, but you, young man, have absolutely nailed it. Well done!" With a little practice, you'll be cooking arctic char like a pro, too!

# ARCTIC CHAR AND RICE NOODLES

in **CURRY BROTH**   serves 4

**Curry Broth**

2 cups seafood stock

2 (13.5-ounce) cans unsweetened coconut milk

1 (1-inch) piece fresh galangal, crushed (see Tip, page 56)

1 (1-inch) piece fresh ginger, crushed

1 teaspoon ground turmeric

1 teaspoon coriander seeds, toasted (see Tip, page 57)

1 tablespoon red curry powder

Pinch of saffron

1 stalk fresh lemongrass

1 tablespoon fish sauce

2 tablespoons fresh lime juice

Kosher salt

**Arctic Char and Rice Noodles**

Vegetable oil, for frying

8 ounces dried rice noodles

3 tablespoons vadouvan spice blend (see Tip, page 67)

1 tablespoon Himalayan black salt

6 tablespoons grapeseed oil

1 cup sliced shiitake mushrooms

2 baby bok choy, quartered lengthwise

Kosher salt and freshly ground black pepper

4 skin-on arctic char fillets, about 4 ounces each

Micro cilantro, for garnish

**1.** Make the curry broth: In a large saucepan, combine the seafood stock, coconut milk, galangal, ginger, turmeric, coriander seeds, curry powder, and saffron. Trim the root end of the lemongrass stalk and cut off the top 2 inches or so. Cut the lemongrass in half lengthwise and peel away and discard any tough, papery layers. Using a rolling pin or a meat mallet, smash the lemongrass to release its flavorful oils. Place the bruised lemongrass in the pot, cutting it again, if needed, to fit. Bring to a simmer over medium-high heat and cook for 20 minutes. Strain the broth through a fine-mesh sieve into a bowl, discard the solids, and stir in the fish sauce and lime juice. Taste and season with salt if needed.

**2.** Make the arctic char and rice noodles: Pour at least 2 inches of vegetable oil into a heavy-bottomed pot. Heat over medium-high heat to 350°F.

*(Continued)*

**3.** Carefully add about one-quarter of the rice noodles to the hot oil and fry until golden, about 1 minute. Transfer to a paper towel–lined plate and sprinkle with the vadouvan and Himalayan salt.

**4.** In a large sauté pan, heat 4 tablespoons of the grapeseed oil over high heat. Add the mushrooms and cook, stirring often, until lightly browned, 3 to 4 minutes. Add the bok choy and cook, stirring, until wilted, about 4 minutes. Remove the pan from the heat and season the vegetables with salt and pepper.

**5.** Bring a large pot of water to a boil. Add the remaining rice noodles and cook for 1 minute. Drain. Transfer to a bowl and stir in ½ cup of the curry broth.

**6.** In a large nonstick pan, heat the remaining 2 tablespoons grapeseed oil over high heat. Season the arctic char fillets with salt and pepper on both sides. Add the fish to the pan, skin-side down, and cook until the skin is golden brown and crisp, about 4 minutes. Flip and cook just until the fish is barely cooked through, about 2 minutes.

**7.** To serve, divide the boiled rice noodles among four shallow bowls. Arrange a few mushroom slices and bok choy pieces over the noodles. Place an arctic char fillet, skin-side up, on top of the vegetables. Garnish with a handful of fried rice noodles and a few sprigs of micro cilantro. Pour the curry broth around the noodles and fish—tableside, if you like!

TIP Toasting whole dried spices is a fantastic way to boost their flavor. Place the spices in a small, dry pan and cook over medium-high heat, stirring often, until very fragrant and lightly browned.

When Logan presented this whole fish baked in a salt crust, the first thing judge Joe Bastianich said was, "This is one of the most unusual entrées we have ever seen in the history of *MasterChef Junior*." All the judges knew Logan had made a bold move, because by baking in a salt crust, Logan was unable to check the doneness of the branzino. He risked baking it too long and ending up with an oversalted, dried-out fish. But, if it worked, it would be incredibly delicious. (For more on salt baking, see page 60.) It turned out that Logan had nailed it—the fish was perfect. Served with a delicious chimichurri sauce, this dish is a real showstopper, so be sure to serve the fish in the salt crust, and then break it open on the table to really impress your guests.

# SALT-BAKED BRANZINO
## and ROASTED BABY VEGETABLES  serves 2

**Salt-Baked Branzino**
2 tablespoons juniper berries
2 tablespoons Sichuan peppercorns
2 tablespoons fennel seeds
2 teaspoons fennel pollen
2 pounds kosher salt
4 large egg whites, beaten
1 whole branzino, gutted and scaled

5 sprigs fresh thyme
2 tablespoons unsalted butter, cut into cubes
1 Meyer lemon, sliced into rounds

**Roasted Baby Vegetables**
½ pound baby pebble potatoes, scrubbed
¼ pound baby carrots

¼ pound baby yellow pattypan squash
¼ pound baby zucchini
2 sprigs fresh thyme
2 tablespoons olive oil
Kosher salt and freshly ground black pepper

Chimichurri (page 30), for serving (optional)

**1.** Preheat the oven to 350°F. Line a baking sheet with parchment paper.

**2.** Make the branzino: Using a spice grinder or small food processor, grind the juniper berries, Sichuan peppercorns, fennel seeds, and fennel pollen until broken down but not completely pulverized. Transfer to a large bowl and stir in the salt and egg whites. Mound half the salt mixture into an even bed on the prepared baking sheet.

**3.** Stuff the branzino with the thyme, butter, and Meyer lemon slices. Place the stuffed branzino over the salt mound and pile the remaining salt mixture

on top of the fish, leaving the tail exposed. Bake for 30 minutes.

**4.** Meanwhile, make the vegetables: In a large bowl, combine the potatoes, carrots, squash, zucchini, thyme, and olive oil. Season with salt and pepper. Arrange the vegetables in a single layer on a baking sheet. Roast until browned, 20 to 25 minutes.

**5.** To serve, present the branzino in the baked salt crust on a platter. Crack the crust with the back of a large spoon, remove the broken crust, and transfer the fish to a plate. Serve the roasted vegetables and the chimichurri (if using) on the side.

## LOGAN'S SALT-BAKING TECHNIQUE

Salt-baking a whole fish is a completely daring and unusual feat that Logan was able to bravely pull off in the finale of Season 2. Funny enough, he learned the technique when he was nine or ten years old by watching a YouTube video of Gordon Ramsay—the very same Gordon Ramsay who is a judge on *MasterChef Junior*! In the video, Gordon demonstrates every step of the salt-baking process, from covering the fish with a salt crust to cracking it open at the table for an extra-grand plating. Logan was so inspired that he asked his mom to buy an affordable whole fish for him to try the technique on at home. His experiment worked! The texture of his first salt-baked fish was amazing and the flavor was perfect, even though the fish wasn't a particularly prized or expensive type.

When Logan encountered branzino for the first time on the show, he decided to risk the challenges of salt-baking and give it a try. "I had never tasted branzino before," he says, "but it was in the *MasterChef* pantry, so it had to be good." Reflecting on that moment, Logan remembers feeling a little worried that the fish might need a lemon-butter sauce served alongside, just in case the fish was dry or lacking in flavor. In the end, he decided to leave off the lemon-butter sauce, letting the clean flavors of the fish speak for themselves. (Sometimes the hardest part of putting together a terrific dish is knowing the importance of restraint!) Logan's salt-baked branzino turned out to be super moist and succulent, and the judges were all so impressed with his mastery of this complicated technique (among other skills) that they pronounced him the winner of Season 2!

Complex and multilayered, this finale main course looks extraordinary, "like a spoonful of diamonds," according to judge Gordon Ramsay. It also tastes remarkable. The judges called it "ridiculously good," "fragrant, bright, and flavorful," and "incredibly moist." Judge Graham Elliot was most impressed by the fact that Addison hadn't just blanched the bok choy, which is the most common way to cook the vegetable, but had sautéed it as well, creating nice caramelization. You could also use this technique on other dark leafy vegetables, such as kale, greens, and even Brussels sprouts!

CONTESTANT:
Addison
—
SEASON 4
FINALE!

# MISO BLACK COD
## in COCONUT-GINGER BROTH  *serves 4*

**Cod and Broth**

Vegetable oil, for frying

1 burdock root (see Tip, page 62), peeled and thinly shaved using a vegetable peeler

Kosher salt

1 cup jade rice

3 tablespoons mirin

3 tablespoons sake

½ cup white miso paste

4 skinless black cod fillets, about 6 ounces each

1 stalk lemongrass

2 tablespoons grapeseed oil

2 tablespoons finely chopped shallot

1 garlic clove, minced

1 (1-inch) piece fresh ginger, peeled and coarsely chopped

2 makrut lime leaves (see Tip, page 63)

2 cups chicken stock

2 cups unsweetened coconut milk

½ lime

**Vegetables**

6 tablespoons grapeseed oil

1 cup shiitake mushrooms, stemmed

1 cup maitake mushrooms (also called hen-of-the-woods)

¼ cup soy sauce

½ cup shelled fresh soybeans

4 baby bok choy, halved lengthwise

¼ cup oyster sauce

1 tablespoon black sesame seeds, toasted (see Tip, page 57)

1 tablespoon white sesame seeds, toasted (see Tip, page 57)

Hot chili oil, for garnish

**1.** Make the cod and broth: Pour at least 2 inches of vegetable oil into a heavy-bottomed pot. Heat over medium-high heat to 350°F.

**2.** Carefully add the shaved burdock to the hot oil and fry until golden, about 3 minutes. Using a slotted spoon, transfer to a paper towel–lined plate, sprinkle with salt, and let cool.

**3.** Bring 1½ cups water to a boil in a medium saucepan. Season the water with salt and add the rice. Reduce the heat to low, cover the pot with a lid, and cook until the rice is tender, 15 to 20 minutes.

**4.** In a small saucepan, bring the mirin, sake, and 2 tablespoons water to a boil. Whisk in the miso

*(Continued)*

TIP Burdock is a slender root vegetable with a meaty texture, sort of like lotus root. Look for it in Asian grocery stores.

paste until completely dissolved. Pour the miso mixture into a shallow dish. Add the black cod fillets and turn to coat. Set aside to marinate at room temperature for at least 30 minutes.

**5.** Meanwhile, trim the root end of the lemongrass stalk and cut off the top 2 inches or so. Cut the lemongrass in half lengthwise and peel away and discard any tough, papery layers. Using a rolling pin or a meat mallet, smash the lemongrass to release the flavorful oils.

**6.** In a medium pot, heat the grapeseed oil over medium heat. Add the lemongrass (cutting it again, if needed, to fit), shallot, garlic, ginger, and makrut lime leaves. Cook, stirring, until the shallot is translucent, 2 to 3 minutes. Pour in the stock and coconut milk and simmer until the mixture thickens slightly, about 20 minutes. Strain through a fine-mesh sieve into a bowl, discard the solids, and season with lime juice and salt. Keep warm.

**7.** Make the vegetables: In a large pan, heat 3 tablespoons of the grapeseed oil over medium-high heat. Add the mushrooms and cook, stirring, until browned, about 4 minutes. Pour in the soy sauce and cook, stirring, until the soy sauce evaporates, 2 to 3 minutes. Stir in the soybeans and remove the pan from the heat.

**8.** Bring a large pot of salted water to a boil. Prepare a bowl of ice water. Add the bok choy to the boiling water and cook until just tender, 2 to 3 minutes. Transfer to the ice bath. Drain and pat dry.

**9.** In a separate large pan, heat the remaining 3 tablespoons grapeseed oil over medium-high heat. Add the blanched bok choy and cook, stirring, until lightly browned, about 5 minutes. Pour in the oyster sauce and stir well. Sprinkle with the black and white sesame seeds.

**10.** Preheat the broiler to high.

**11.** Transfer the marinated cod to a baking dish. Broil until the fish is cooked through and flaky, 8 to 10 minutes.

**12.** To serve, place a heaping tablespoon of steamed rice in each of four shallow bowls. Place a piece of miso black cod next to the rice and arrange a heaping tablespoon of mushrooms next to the cod. Place 2 bok choy halves next to the mushrooms. Scatter the fried burdock over the fish and vegetables. Spoon the coconut-ginger broth around the bowl and garnish with drops of the chili oil.

TIP Makrut lime leaves are an important ingredient in Southeast Asian cuisine. They have an intense zesty aroma because they come from the makrut lime tree, a citrus fruit tree native to tropical Asia. You can buy them in Asian grocery stores—if you don't see the fresh leaves near the vegetables and fruits, check the freezer section.

The incredibly popular fish taco can be made hundreds of ways. But in the *MasterChef Junior* kitchen, you can be sure there will be a surprise twist. Sure enough, when Molly presented these during her audition, she garnished her fish tacos with one unexpected ingredient—pomegranate seeds! They are pops of delicious sweetness and look fantastic sprinkled over the fish. Best of all, Molly's creativity reminds us to never stop experimenting and trying new things in the kitchen.

# FISH TACOS WITH GUACAMOLE

serves 4

1 pound Atlantic cod fillet, cut into 4 portions
3 tablespoons olive oil
Juice of 3½ limes, plus lime wedges for serving
2 ripe avocados, pitted and peeled

2 tablespoons minced onion
Vegetable oil, for frying
Kosher salt and freshly ground black pepper
1½ cups all-purpose flour
4 white corn tortillas, warmed

½ cup Mexican crema
½ cup shredded red cabbage
½ cup shredded green cabbage
¼ cup fresh cilantro leaves
¼ cup pomegranate seeds

**1.** Place the cod in a shallow dish, pour in the olive oil and the juice of 3 of the limes, and let the fish marinate for 15 minutes.

**2.** Meanwhile, mash the avocados in a medium bowl. Add the onion and the juice of the remaining ½ lime and mix well.

**3.** Pour at least 2 inches of vegetable oil into a heavy-bottomed pot. Heat over medium-high heat to 350°F.

**4.** Remove the cod from the marinade, pat dry, and season with salt and pepper on all sides. Dredge the cod in the flour, shaking off any excess. Working in batches, carefully lower the floured cod into the hot oil and fry until golden brown, 3 to 4 minutes. Transfer to a paper towel–lined plate and let cool slightly.

**5.** Use two forks to break the cod up into large, flaky pieces. Divide among the tortillas, drizzle with crema, and top with shredded red and green cabbage, cilantro, and pomegranate seeds. Serve with the guacamole and lime wedges on the side.

"I started cooking when I was three or four. I was working with my mom in the kitchen making pancakes, and I spilled all the eggs I was mixing all over myself and the floor and started to get upset. My mom told me that it was okay and that we could just start again, and they turned out great. From that, I learned not to make a big deal out of a mistake, because cooking is just an experiment and you have to have fun with it." —Jasmine

Monkfish have distinctive scowling faces and large teeth! Don't be fooled by their appearance, though, because fillets cut from their tail are firm, white, and delicious. Just be aware that monkfish is quite lean and can easily dry out if overcooked. Here, Jasmine paired the fish with salty pancetta, which actually appears twice in this dish.

# VADOUVAN-SPICED MONKFISH

## with PANCETTA LENTILS serves 4

½ cup diced pancetta, plus 4 thin slices pancetta

2 medium shallots, finely chopped

2 tablespoons minced garlic

1 cup white wine

8 cups chicken stock

1¼ cups (2½ sticks) unsalted butter

Kosher salt and freshly ground black pepper

2 medium zucchini, very thinly sliced

1 pint cherry tomatoes, halved

2 cups lentils

Zest and juice of 1 lemon

2 tablespoons grapeseed oil

4 skinless monkfish fillets, about 6 ounces each

4 sprigs fresh thyme

3 tablespoons vadouvan spice blend (see Tip)

**1.** Preheat the oven to 450°F. Line a baking sheet with parchment paper.

**2.** Place the pancetta slices in a single layer without overlapping on the prepared baking sheet. Bake until crisp, 16 to 18 minutes.

**3.** In a medium saucepan, combine the shallots, garlic, wine, and 2 cups of the stock. Bring to a boil over medium-high heat and cook until reduced by half, about 20 minutes. Gradually whisk in 1 cup of the butter until melted and incorporated. Season with salt and pepper.

**4.** Place the zucchini and tomatoes in a large bowl. Season with salt and pepper and some of the butter sauce and toss to coat.

**5.** In a large saucepan, combine the lentils and remaining 6 cups stock. Bring to a boil over high heat. Meanwhile, in a small sauté pan, cook the diced pancetta over medium-high heat until crisp,

about 5 minutes. Transfer the pancetta to the pan with the lentils. Cook the lentils until tender, 25 to 30 minutes. Drain. Season with salt, pepper, and the lemon zest and juice.

**6.** In a large nonstick pan, heat the grapeseed oil over medium-high heat. Season the monkfish with salt and pepper and add to the pan. Cook until browned on the first side, about 3 minutes. Add the remaining ¼ cup butter, the thyme, and the vadouvan. Flip the monkfish and cook on the second side until just opaque throughout, about 1 minute.

**7.** To serve, spoon the pancetta lentils into four shallow bowls. Place the vandouvan-spiced monkfish over the lentils and arrange the zucchini and tomatoes around the fish. Spoon some reserved butter sauce around the bowl. Top with 1 crisp pancetta slice.

TIP Vadouvan is an Indian spice blend that typically includes dried onion and garlic, fenugreek, cumin, and mustard seeds.

This rich yellow curry dish features prawns two ways. First, whole prawns (with their heads!) cook directly in the curry, infusing the sauce with their sweet, briny flavor. Second, dumplings filled with a mixture of prawns, chives, and cream are added to the curry just before serving. Judge Joe Bastianich congratulated Dara on cooking such a terrific, restaurant-quality dish, telling her, "I'd pay forty-five dollars for this!"

# THAI PRAWN CURRY
## with PRAWN DUMPLINGS  serves 4

1 (13.5-ounce) can unsweetened coconut milk
2 tablespoons chicken stock
¼ cup yellow curry paste
1 large carrot, thinly sliced
2 makrut lime leaves (see Tip, page 63)

1½ teaspoons fish sauce
¼ cup Thai basil, leaves and stems separated
12 large prawns, head on
¼ cup heavy cream
1 tablespoon chopped fresh chives

1 (12-ounce) package wonton wrappers
½ cup snow peas, trimmed
4 ounces shimeji mushrooms (also known as beach mushrooms)
Kosher salt

1. In a large saucepan, combine the coconut milk, stock, and curry paste. Bring to a boil over medium-high heat and cook, stirring continuously, until smooth, about 1 minute. Add the carrot, makrut lime leaves, fish sauce, and Thai basil stems, reserving the basil leaves for garnishing the finished dish. Reduce the heat to low, cover the pan, and cook until slightly thickened, 30 minutes.

2. Meanwhile, cut off and discard the heads of 6 of the prawns, and remove the shells as well. Place the shelled prawns in a food processor and add the cream and chives. Blend until smooth. Place a heaping teaspoon of prawn purée in the center of a wonton wrapper. Dab a wet finger around the edges of the wrapper, and then fold the wrapper around the filling, pressing the edges to seal. Repeat with the remaining wrappers and filling.

3. Uncover the pan of curry sauce and add the snow peas and mushrooms. Cook, stirring occasionally, over low heat until the peas and mushrooms are tender, about 5 minutes. Season with salt. Discard the lime leaves and basil stems. Keep warm.

4. Bring a large pot of water to a boil. Add the prawn dumplings and boil until cooked through, about 3 minutes. Using a slotted spoon, transfer the dumplings to a plate.

5. Add the remaining 6 prawns to the curry sauce and cook over low heat, stirring often, until the prawns turn pink, about 4 minutes.

6. To serve, spoon the Thai prawn curry into four shallow bowls, arranging the whole prawns in the center with their heads poking up. Divide the prawn dumplings among the bowls and garnish with the reserved basil leaves.

Nate was so proud of the plating of this dish that he was presenting to the judges that he joked, "I think it looks great. I would probably marry it, if I had the chance!" It turned out that judge Christina Tosi loved the combination of Asian flavors going on here—the yellowtail's soy marinade and the sweet-sour rice vinegar dressing on the Cucumber and Tomato Salad (page 172), which Nate had arranged on the side. "This is the very best fish dish I've had in the *MasterChef Junior* kitchen," she said.

# SOY-MARINATED YELLOWTAIL

## with SAUTÉED GREEN BEANS and MUSHROOMS   serves 4

¼ cup soy sauce

½ cup rice vinegar

2 tablespoons sriracha sauce

1 tablespoon sesame seeds

1 tablespoon chopped fresh chives, plus more for garnish

4 yellowtail fillets, about 6 ounces each

Kosher salt

½ pound green beans, trimmed

2 tablespoons unsalted butter

6 tablespoons grapeseed oil

2 cups button mushrooms, chopped

Freshly ground black pepper

**1.** In a wide, shallow dish, whisk together the soy sauce, vinegar, sriracha, sesame seeds, and chives. Add the yellowtail fillets and let marinate at room temperature for about 30 minutes.

**2.** Meanwhile, bring a large pot of salted water to a boil. Prepare a bowl of ice water. Add the green beans to the boiling water and cook until tender, 3 to 4 minutes. Using a slotted spoon, transfer the beans to the ice bath. Let cool, then drain.

**3.** In a large sauté pan, heat the butter and 2 table-spoons of the grapeseed oil over medium heat. Add the mushrooms and cook, stirring, until browned, about 6 minutes. Add the blanched green beans

and toss to coat. Remove the pan from the heat and season with salt and pepper.

**4.** In a large nonstick sauté pan, heat the remaining 4 tablespoons grapeseed oil over medium heat. Lift the yellowtail fillets out of the marinade and place them in the pan. Sear until browned on two sides, 3 to 4 minutes per side. Transfer to a plate and let rest for a few minutes.

**5.** To serve, arrange some sautéed green beans and mushrooms in the center of each of four plates. Place a soy-marinated yellowtail fillet on top and garnish with chives.

# FOUR WAYS TO COOK FISH PERFECTLY

*MasterChef Junior* contestants are no strangers to making fish! And the range of techniques they've mastered is impressive. They fry, sear, broil, and even wrap in puff pastry and then bake fish of all kinds. When you're preparing it at home, make sure to start with pristinely fresh fish—it should smell salty and clean, like the ocean. The type of fish matters less than its freshness. For example, salmon would be a fine substitute for arctic char, and any white, firm-fleshed fish could stand in for black cod. If you aren't sure about a specific substitution, ask your fishmonger for his or her recommendation. And, as for what to do with fresh fish, here are four techniques for cooking fish fillets perfectly every time:

1) **Broil:** Preheat the broiler to high. After seasoning the fillets, place them skin-side down on a baking sheet and broil until just barely opaque all the way through, 7 to 10 minutes. Discard the skin before serving.

2) **Poach in Olive Oil:** In a large sauté pan with at least 3-inch-high sides, warm 1 quart olive oil over low heat until the oil registers 120°F on an instant-read thermometer. Cut 1 lemon into thin slices and add to the oil while it heats up. Season 4 fish fillets (each about 4 ounces) with salt and pepper on both sides. Carefully add the fish to the warm oil, making sure the fillets are completely submerged. (If they are not, add more oil as needed.) Poach for 10 minutes. Transfer the fish to a wire rack and allow the excess oil to drip off for a few minutes.

3) **Pan Sear:** In a large nonstick pan, heat 2 tablespoons grapeseed oil over high heat. Season the fillets with salt and pepper on both sides. Add the fish to the pan, skin-side down, and cook until the skin is golden brown and crisp, 2 to 4 minutes. Flip and cook on the second side just until the fish is barely cooked through, 2 to 4 minutes.

4) **Fry:** Pour at least 2 inches of vegetable oil into a heavy-bottomed pot and heat the oil to 350°F. Pat the fillets dry and season with salt and pepper on all sides. Dredge the fish in all-purpose flour (or try different kinds of breading for the crust, such as cornmeal or finely ground saltine crackers), shaking off any excess. Carefully lower the floured fish into the hot oil and fry until golden brown, about 5 minutes. Transfer to a paper towel–lined plate and let cool slightly before serving.

And here's a bonus! For a fifth showstopping way to cook fish, see Logan's technique for salt-baking a whole fish on page 60. Although he used branzino, this amazing trick would also work really well with other whole, scaled, and gutted medium-size fishes, like orata and red snapper.

A true Louisiana girl at heart, Avery grew up on étouffée. This thickened seafood stew from the Cajun and Creole cuisines of Louisiana is nearly the definition of comfort food: warm, packed with flavor, and incredibly satisfying. It can be made with any type of shellfish, but Avery chose to make her version with the most traditional ingredient—crayfish, which people in Louisiana call crawfish. Feel free to put your own spin on this dish by using your favorite type of shellfish, or a combination of shrimp, crab, scallops, and clams, adding up to a total of one pound.

# CRAWFISH ÉTOUFFÉE

serves 4

Kosher salt
1½ cups long-grain white rice
¼ cup all-purpose flour
4 tablespoons (½ stick) unsalted butter
1 cup finely chopped onion

½ cup chopped celery
½ cup chopped green bell pepper
1 pound crawfish tail meat
1 teaspoon minced garlic
¼ teaspoon cayenne

1 bay leaf
Freshly ground black pepper
¼ cup thinly sliced scallions, white and light green parts
2 tablespoons chopped fresh flat-leaf parsley

**1.** Bring 3 cups water to a boil in a medium saucepan. Season with salt and add the rice. Reduce the heat to low, cover the pot, and cook until the rice is tender, 12 to 15 minutes.

**2.** Meanwhile, in a small saucepan, whisk together the flour and 1½ cups water. Cook over low heat, whisking, until thickened, 6 to 8 minutes.

**3.** In a large sauté pan, melt the butter over medium heat. Add the onion, celery, and bell pepper and cook, stirring, until softened, 3 to 4 minutes. Add

the crawfish, garlic, cayenne, and bay leaf and cook for 4 to 5 minutes more. Using a wooden spoon, stir in the flour mixture. Season with salt and black pepper. Reduce the heat to low and cook for a few minutes more. If the étouffée is too thick, add water, 1 tablespoon at a time, to thin it to your desired consistency.

**4.** Just before serving, stir in the scallions and parsley. Discard the bay leaf. Spoon some rice into each of four shallow bowls and top with the étouffée.

With a stunning combination of green, yellow, and white ingredients, this dish looks as impressive as it tastes. The scallops are great on their own, but if you're serving them over the Lemon Risotto (page 169), as Tae-Ho did in Season 4, you'll need to make it before searing the scallops. The smoky and slightly spicy jalapeño-poblano salsa can also be made ahead of time. Other great dishes to serve with the scallops are Broccoli Rabe Purée (page 165) or Grilled Corn Succotash (page 170).

CONTESTANT:
Tae-Ho
—
SEASON 4

# SEARED SCALLOPS
## with JALAPEÑO-POBLANO SALSA serves 4

**Jalapeño-Poblano Salsa**
2 jalapeños
1 poblano pepper
½ red onion, chopped
2 garlic cloves
1 cup fresh cilantro
½ cup rice vinegar

1 teaspoon ground coriander
3 tablespoons olive oil
Juice of 1 lemon
Kosher salt

6 large Brussels sprouts
2 tablespoons olive oil

12 large scallops
Kosher salt and freshly ground
    black pepper
2 tablespoons grapeseed oil
1 red, golden, or candy cane beet
Lemon Risotto (page 169;
    optional)

**1.** Make the jalapeño-poblano salsa: Using tongs, hold the jalapeños and poblano, one at a time, over a direct flame on a gas stovetop and char all sides, turning to cook evenly. (Alternatively, char under a broiler.) Transfer to a plastic bag, close the bag, and let the peppers steam for 5 to 10 minutes. Remove the peppers from the bag, peel off the skins, and discard the stems and seeds. Place the peeled peppers in a blender or food processor. Add the onion, garlic, cilantro, vinegar, coriander, olive oil, and lemon juice. Blend until smooth. Transfer to a medium bowl and season with salt.

**2.** Trim the bottoms of the Brussels sprouts and peel each sprout into individual leaves, trimming more of the bottom as needed. In a large pan, heat the olive oil over medium-high heat. Add the Brussels sprout leaves and cook, stirring, until wilted, about 1 minute. Transfer to a plate.

**3.** Season the scallops with salt and pepper on both sides. Return the large pan to the stove over high heat. Add the grapeseed oil and about half the scallops. Sear the scallops until browned on two sides, about 3 minutes per side. Transfer to a plate and repeat with the remaining scallops.

**4.** Using a vegetable peeler, remove the skin from the beet; discard the skin. Continue peeling to create very thin petals of raw beet.

**5.** To serve, spoon the risotto, if using, into four shallow bowls and top each with 3 scallops and the salsa. Scatter the Brussels sprouts and beet petals over the top.

When cooking alligator meat, follow Cory's lead and use lots of different spices to create a bold dish with a touch of heat. Including grilled pineapple is a brilliant way to balance the spiciness with sweetness. Although alligator meat is common in the South, it's not as easy to find in other parts of the country; look for it in specialty markets or buy it online.

CONTESTANT:
Cory
—
SEASON 3

# ALLIGATOR STIR-FRY
## with GRILLED PINEAPPLE  serves 4

½ small pineapple, peeled and cut into rounds

5 tablespoons grapeseed oil, plus more for brushing

1 pound alligator meat, finely chopped

Kosher salt and freshly ground black pepper

1 tablespoon toasted sesame oil

½ cup chopped carrot

1 cup chopped onion

2 cups coarsely chopped broccoli

1 cup fresh corn kernels

½ jalapeño, finely chopped

3 black garlic cloves (see Tip), minced

½ teaspoon Chinese five-spice powder

¼ teaspoon freshly grated nutmeg

¼ cup soy sauce

1 tablespoon fish sauce

1 teaspoon black sesame seeds

4 large eggs

Steamed rice, made without rose water (see page 89)

1. Heat a grill to high or a grill pan over high heat.

2. Brush the pineapple rounds with grapeseed oil on both sides. Grill, flipping once, until lightly charred, about 2 minutes per side. Transfer to a plate and let cool slightly. Finely chop about 1 cup of the grilled pineapple and set aside 4 rounds for serving.

3. In a wok or large pan, heat 3 tablespoons of the grapeseed oil over high heat. Add the alligator meat and cook, stirring, until browned, about 8 minutes. Transfer to a plate and season with salt and pepper.

4. To the wok, add the sesame oil, carrot, and onion and cook, stirring, until softened, about 2 minutes. Add the broccoli, corn, jalapeño, black garlic, Chinese five-spice, and nutmeg and cook, stirring, until the vegetables brown, about 5 minutes. Stir in the soy sauce, fish sauce, sesame seeds, and the cooked alligator meat and chopped pineapple. Season with salt and pepper.

5. In a large pan, heat the remaining 2 tablespoons grapeseed oil over medium-high heat. Crack in the eggs, making sure they don't touch, and fry until the whites are set, about 5 minutes.

6. To serve, spoon some steamed rice in the center of each of four plates. Top each with the alligator stir-fry and a fried egg. Garnish with a grilled pineapple round.

TIP Black garlic, an ingredient used in Asian cuisines, gets its dark color from a weeks-long cooking process. It tastes syrupy and sweet, sort of like balsamic vinegar. Look for it in Asian grocery stores.

Like jewels on display, a stunningly beautiful collection of seafood comes together in this elegant dish. Calamari tentacles, baby scallops the size of silver dollars, and thin slices of razor clam surround a seared red snapper fillet, and a flavorful shellfish broth poured over everything ties together these many flavors of the sea. You could certainly use any combination of fresh seafood that you prefer, but keep in mind that a mixture of textures—tender, chewy, and flaky—is ideal.

# SEAFOOD AND RAINBOW CHARD
## in SHELLFISH BROTH  serves 4

### Rainbow Chard

Kosher salt

1 large bunch rainbow chard

2 tablespoons grapeseed oil

2 tablespoons unsalted butter

1 tablespoon finely chopped shallot

1 tablespoon minced garlic

Freshly ground black pepper

### Seafood

4 skin-on red snapper fillets, about 4 ounces each

Kosher salt and freshly ground black pepper

6 tablespoons grapeseed oil

20 small calamari tentacles

20 baby scallops

4 razor clams, cleaned and cut into ¼-inch slices

4 sprigs fresh thyme

1 tablespoon finely chopped shallot

1 tablespoon minced garlic

½ cup white wine

1 lemon, quartered

### Shellfish Broth

1 cup shellfish stock

¼ cup extra-virgin olive oil

¼ cup finely chopped red bell pepper

¼ cup finely chopped yellow bell pepper

2 tablespoons chopped fresh chives

Kosher salt

8 (1-inch-long) pieces sea bean (see Tip, page 19)

20 fresh nasturtium leaves (see Tip, page 78)

¼ cup chopped fresh chives

1. Make the rainbow chard: Bring a large pot of salted water to a boil. Prepare a bowl of ice water.

2. Pull or cut the chard leaves off the stems. Coarsely chop the leaves and thinly slice the stems. Reserve the stems. Add the chard leaves to the boiling water and cook until just tender, 2 to 3 minutes. Immediately transfer to the ice water, let cool, and then drain.

3. In a large sauté pan, heat the grapeseed oil and butter over medium-high heat. Add the shallot and garlic and cook until softened, about 2 minutes. Add the reserved chard stems and cook, stirring often, until softened, about 4 minutes. Add the blanched chard leaves and stir until heated through. Season with salt and black pepper.

*(Continued)*

**4.** Make the seafood: Season the red snapper fillets with salt and black pepper and use a knife to score the skin in a crosshatch pattern. In a large nonstick pan, heat 3 tablespoons of the grapeseed oil set over medium-high heat. Place the snapper skin-side down in the pan and cook until the skin is crisp, 3 to 4 minutes. Flip and cook on the second side for 1 minute. Transfer the snapper to a plate. Add the remaining 3 tablespoons grapeseed oil to the pan. Add the calamari and scallops and cook, stirring, for 1 minute. Add the razor clams, thyme, shallot, and garlic and cook until all the seafood is lightly browned and cooked through, 4 to 5 minutes. Add the wine and a few squeezes of lemon juice. Cook, stirring and scraping the bottom of the pan with a wooden spoon, until the wine has reduced slightly, about 2 minutes. Remove the pan from the heat and season with salt and black pepper.

**5.** Make the shellfish broth: Bring the stock to a simmer in a small saucepan over medium heat. Remove the pan from the heat and add the olive oil, red bell pepper, yellow bell pepper, and chives. Season with salt, if needed.

**6.** To serve, arrange a heaping tablespoon of the rainbow chard mixture in the center of each of four shallow bowls. Place 1 snapper fillet on top of the chard and arrange the rest of the seafood around the snapper. Spoon a few tablespoons of the broth into each bowl. Garnish with sea beans, nasturtium leaves, and chives.

TIP Nasturtium leaves come from the beautiful plant of the same name with sunny yellow-orange flowers. You may have seen it growing in your neighborhood—it's one of the most popular garden plants! The leaves and flower petals are edible and have a terrific peppery taste, sort of like arugula or watercress. You can also buy nasturtium leaves at some grocery stores.

"What inspires me in the kitchen is the quest to make things out of what I have in my pantry and to make them delicious and something that represents me—sweet, Southern, savory, and Caribbean. Once I've done that, I know my meal is going to be great. And it's incredibly fun!" —Jasmine

In her version of West Indian curry, Jasmine honors tradition by including some of the classic flavors of the Caribbean: chile, cilantro, pepper, and citrus. At the same time, she makes it uniquely hers in many ways, including garnishing with finger lime, a tiny citrus relative native to Australia. Finger limes are filled with caviar-shaped bubbles of zesty juice, and they add fun pops of flavor to this stunning dish.

CONTESTANT:
Jasmine
—
SEASON 5
FINALE!

# WEST INDIAN LOBSTER CURRY

`serves 4`

### Curry Sauce
1 tablespoon grapeseed oil
1 red bell pepper, chopped
1 green bell pepper, chopped
2 celery stalks, chopped
1 small yellow onion, chopped
½ serrano chile, sliced
3 tablespoons tomato paste
2 tablespoons red curry powder
2 tablespoons white rum
2 (5.5-ounce) cans mixed vegetable juice, such as V8
2 cups unsweetened coconut milk
1 quart seafood or shellfish stock
Juice of 2 key limes
6 sprigs fresh cilantro
2 tablespoons unsalted butter

### Lobster
Kosher salt
4 lobster tails, shell on
1 cup (2 sticks) unsalted butter
1 tablespoon jerk seasoning
2 garlic cloves, crushed

### Vegetables
2 orange sweet potatoes, peeled and diced
2 purple sweet potatoes, peeled and diced
1 cup shelled English peas
2 tablespoons unsalted butter
1 tablespoon dark brown sugar
Kosher salt

8 yellow cherry tomatoes
2 tablespoons chili oil
4 finger limes, rinds removed
¼ cup chopped fresh chives
¼ cup micro cilantro

1. Make the curry sauce: Heat a large pan over medium heat. Add the grapeseed oil, red and green bell peppers, celery, onion, and serrano and cook, stirring, until tender, 5 minutes. Add the tomato paste and red curry powder and cook, stirring, for 2 minutes. Pour in the rum and simmer until the liquid has mostly evaporated, about 1 minute. Add the vegetable juice, coconut milk, stock, key lime juice, and cilantro. Reduce the heat to low and simmer until the curry sauce has thickened and coats the back of a spoon, about 45 minutes.

2. Meanwhile, make the lobster: Bring a medium pot of salted water to a boil. Prepare a bowl of ice water.

*(Continued)*

Add the lobster tails to the boiling water and cook for 5 minutes. Transfer the lobster to the ice water (leave the pot of salted water on the stove, with the heat turned off). Remove and discard the shells.

**3.** In a medium sauté pan, melt the butter set over medium heat. Add the jerk seasoning, garlic, and lobster tails. Cook, spooning the butter over the lobster meat frequently, until the lobster is cooked through, about 4 minutes. Transfer the lobster to a plate and let cool slightly.

**4.** Make the vegetables: Bring the pot of water used for the lobster to a boil. Prepare two separate bowls of ice water. Add the orange and purple sweet potatoes to the boiling water, cook for 1 minute, and then transfer to one bowl of ice water. Add the peas to the water, cook for 1 minute, and then transfer to the second bowl of ice water.

**5.** In a large pan, melt the butter over medium heat. Drain the vegetables and pat them dry with a clean kitchen towel. Add the blanched sweet potatoes to the pan and cook, stirring occasionally, until tender, about 3 minutes. Add the blanched peas and brown sugar and cook, stirring, until the sugar dissolves. Remove the pan from the heat. Season the vegetables with salt.

**6.** Just before serving, strain the sauce through a fine-mesh sieve, discarding the solids. Return the sauce to a pot, add the butter, and heat gently until the butter melts.

**7.** To serve, arrange 1 lobster tail in the center of each of four shallow bowls. Spoon the curry sauce around the lobster. Scatter the cooked vegetables around the lobster in the sauce. Garnish with cherry tomatoes, chili oil, finger limes, chives, and micro cilantro.

# MEAT & POULTRY

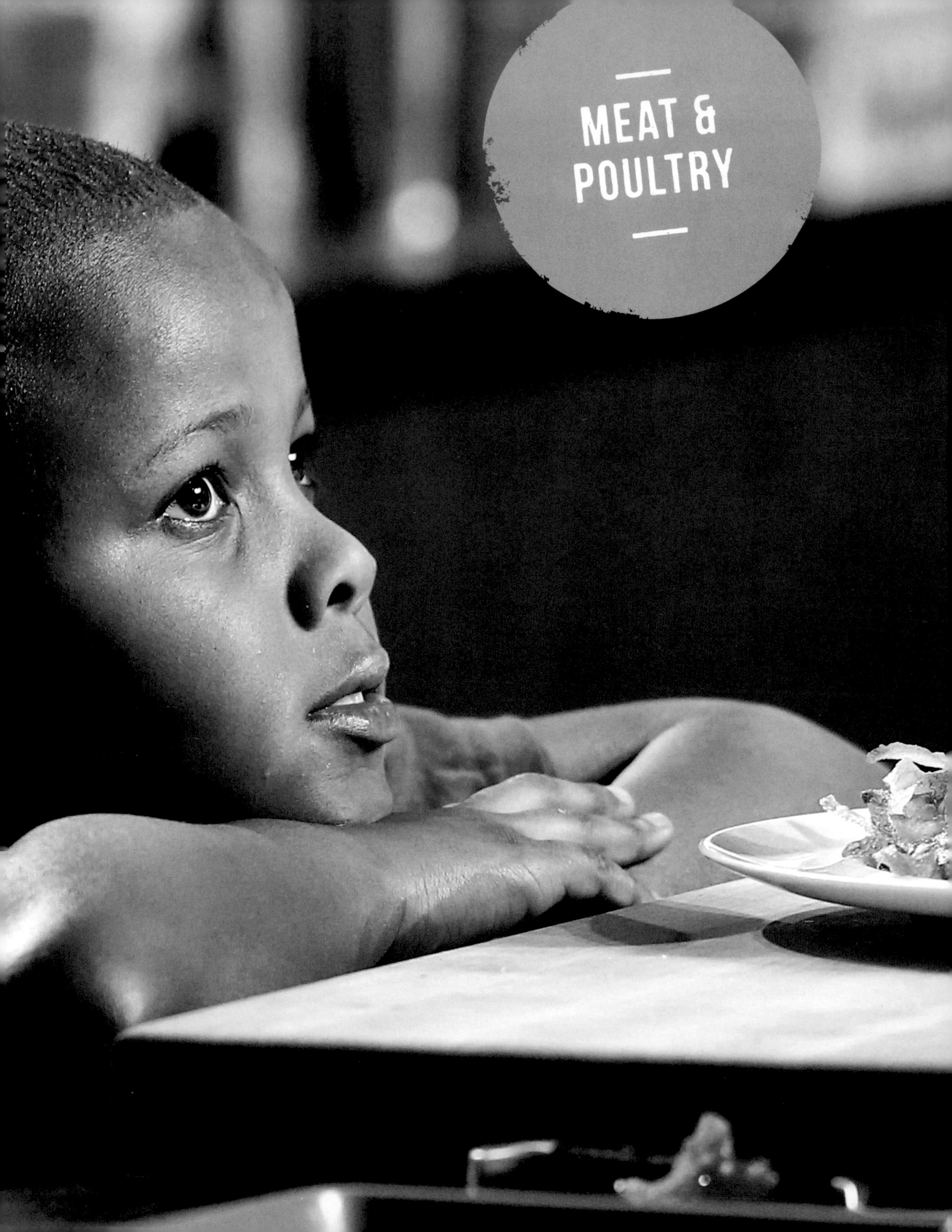

For a special Mystery Box Challenge, we asked judge Christina Tosi's mother, Greta, to put together the ingredients inside the box. She selected all the foods Christina ate as a child: strawberries, chocolate chips, chicken breasts, three types of cereal, and a few other sweet ingredients. Many of the contestants chose to make a dessert, but Zac decided to be a little different and prepared this simple savory dish. To serve it just like he did, don't forget the Sautéed Broccolini (page 168)! Or mix it up and try Parmesan Mashed Potatoes (page 156) on the side.

# PAN-SEARED CHICKEN
## with SHOESTRING FRIES  *serves 4*

1 large Yukon Gold potato
3 tablespoons grapeseed oil
Kosher salt and freshly ground
  black pepper

Canola oil, for frying
4 boneless, skinless chicken
  breasts
7 tablespoons unsalted butter

9 sprigs fresh thyme
2 cups chicken stock
¼ cup heavy cream
Fresh cilantro leaves, for garnish

**1.** Peel the potato and use a spiral cutter to cut the potato into thin noodles. Cut the noodles crosswise into matchstick-length pieces. (Alternatively, use a knife to cut the potato into matchsticks.) Pat the potatoes dry, toss them with 1 tablespoon of the grapeseed oil, and season with salt and pepper.

**2.** Pour at least 2 inches of canola oil into a large, heavy-bottomed pot. Heat over medium-high heat to 350°F. Add the potato pieces and fry until golden brown and crisp, 2 to 3 minutes. Using a slotted spoon, transfer the fries to a paper towel–lined plate and let cool.

**3.** Preheat the oven to 350°F.

**4.** Season the chicken breasts with salt and pepper. In a large, oven-safe pan, heat the remaining 2 tablespoons grapeseed oil over medium-high heat.

Add the chicken and cook until browned on both sides, 2 to 3 minutes per side. Add 4 tablespoons of the butter and 6 sprigs of the thyme, spooning the butter over the chicken breasts as it melts. Transfer the pan to the oven and roast until the chicken is cooked through, about 5 minutes.

**5.** In a medium saucepan, bring the stock and the remaining 3 sprigs thyme to a simmer over medium-high heat. Whisk in the cream and return to a simmer. Remove the pan from the heat and whisk in the remaining 3 tablespoons butter. Season with salt and pepper.

**6.** To serve, place a chicken breast in the center of each of four plates. Spoon the cream sauce over the chicken and garnish with cilantro. Serve with the crispy shoestring fries.

This memorable challenge presented contestants with endless "spicy," "smelly," and "wrinkly" ingredients. Addison's response? "If you can't beat them, then join them!" Choosing to use many of the unusual ingredients, Addison combined them all into one winning soup. Clever ideas, like flavoring the steamed rice with rose water, put her dish at the top of the class. Don't forget to let the ingredients inspire you! Sometimes it's more fun to let them lead and see where they take you.

CONTESTANT:
Addison

— SEASON 4 —

# TOM KA GAI WITH CHICKEN MEATBALLS

serves 4

### Rice
1 tablespoon rose water
1 cup jasmine rice
1 teaspoon kosher salt

### Soup
3 tablespoons canola oil
4 garlic cloves, sliced
3 makrut lime leaves (see Tip, page 63)
1 (1-inch) piece fresh ginger, peeled and sliced
1 stalk lemongrass, bottom 4 inches only, quartered lengthwise
2 (15-ounce) cans unsweetened coconut milk
4 cups chicken stock

2 tablespoons ground ginger
3 tablespoons fish sauce
3 tablespoons red curry paste
3 tablespoons sugar
Juice of 3 limes
1 tablespoon kosher salt
1 teaspoon freshly ground black pepper

### Vegetables
3 tablespoons grapeseed oil
6 oyster mushrooms, sliced
1 cup sliced button mushrooms
4 baby bok choy, bottoms trimmed and leaves separated
2 red bell peppers, thinly sliced
Kosher salt and freshly ground black pepper

### Chicken Meatballs
½ cup corn nuts
1 boneless, skinless chicken breast, cut into 1-inch pieces
2 boneless, skinless chicken thighs, cut into 1-inch pieces
½ cup panko bread crumbs
2 scallions, white and light green parts, cut into 1-inch pieces
4 garlic cloves, sliced
1 (1-inch) piece fresh ginger, peeled and sliced
Kosher salt and freshly ground black pepper

Finely grated lime zest, for garnish

1. Make the rice: In a medium saucepan, combine the rose water, rice, salt, and 1½ cups water and bring to a boil over high heat. Reduce the heat to low, cover the pan, and simmer until the rice is almost tender, 10 minutes. Remove the pan from the heat and let sit, covered, for 15 minutes.

2. Make the soup: In a large pot, heat the canola oil over medium-high heat. Add the garlic, makrut lime leaves, fresh ginger, and lemongrass and cook, stirring, until the garlic browns, 5 minutes. Add the coconut milk, stock, ground ginger, fish sauce, red

(Continued)

curry paste, sugar, lime juice, salt, and black pepper. Bring to a simmer and cook until thickened and reduced slightly, about 20 minutes.

**3.** Strain the liquid through a fine-mesh sieve into a large bowl, discard the solids, and then return the soup to the pot. Bring the soup to a very low simmer and keep warm.

**4.** Make the vegetables: In a large pan, heat the grapeseed oil over medium-high heat. Add the mushrooms, bok choy, and bell pepper. Season with salt and black pepper. Cook, stirring often, just until tender, 3 to 4 minutes. Transfer to a plate.

**5.** Make the chicken meatballs: In a food processor, grind the corn nuts to a coarse powder. Add the chicken breast and thighs, bread crumbs, scallions, garlic, fresh ginger, 2 teaspoons of salt, and

2 teaspoons of black pepper to the food processor. Blend until a smooth paste forms. Use a spoon and your hands to shape the mixture into golf ball–size meatballs.

**6.** Heat the pan you cooked the vegetables in over medium-high heat. Add as many meatballs as will fit in a single layer and cook, flipping once or twice, until browned and cooked through, about 2 minutes per side. Transfer the cooked meatballs to the soup. Repeat with the remaining meatballs.

**7.** A few minutes before serving, add the cooked vegetables to the soup and simmer until heated through. To serve, place a scoop of steamed rice in the center of each of four bowls. Spoon the soup around the rice, making sure to include a few meatballs, and garnish with lime zest.

"Practice your knife skills.
They can really elevate anything
you cook at home. Not only is it
impressive, but it also makes the
end result look better." —Alexander

Using just a knife (and some serious skills!), Samuel turned cucumbers into noodles. He then dressed them with an easy arugula pesto and coiled them into a bundle for an impressive presentation. The cucumber pasta may be the most visually striking element of this dish, but it was the perfectly cooked, full-flavored duck breast that most impressed judge Gordon Ramsay.

# FIVE-SPICE DUCK BREAST

## with CUCUMBER "PASTA"  serves 4

2 cups arugula
¼ cup olive oil
Kosher salt and freshly ground
    black pepper

6 Persian cucumbers
½ cup (1 stick) unsalted butter,
    melted

2 tablespoons Chinese five-spice
    powder
4 skin-on duck breasts

**1.** Preheat the oven to 375°F.

**2.** In a blender or a food processor, purée the arugula and olive oil until completely smooth. Season with salt and pepper.

**3.** Slice the cucumbers lengthwise as thinly as possible, and then cut each strip lengthwise into thin "noodles." (Alternatively, you can use a spiralizer to cut the cucumbers.) Toss the sliced cucumber with the arugula pesto in a bowl and set aside to marinate for 15 to 20 minutes.

**4.** Meanwhile, mix together the butter and Chinese five-spice. Score the skin of the duck breasts in a crosshatch pattern. Generously season the duck with salt and pepper on both sides.

**5.** Heat a large pan over medium heat. Place the duck breasts skin-side down in the pan and cook until the skin is evenly browned, about 5 minutes. Flip and cook on the second side for 1 minute. Transfer the duck breasts to a baking sheet and brush the spiced butter across the skin sides.

**6.** Roast the duck breasts until the internal temperature reaches 165°F for medium, 10 to 12 minutes. Remove the pan from the oven and let rest for 10 minutes.

**7.** To serve, slice the duck breasts on an angle. Place the slices on one side of a plate and arrange the cucumber "pasta" in a tight bundle on the other side of the plate.

Pork chops can be tricky! Unlike beef, which can be served at a range of temperatures, pork must be cooked perfectly to ensure it's safe to eat, but it can be easy to overcook. In this recipe, Natalie rose to the challenge, relying on the expert technique of starting on the stove and finishing in the oven, which ensures a nice, browned crust and juicy inside. Pairing pork chops with root vegetables and a mustard sauce creates a classic fall or winter dish, but by mixing apples with carrots, Natalie deepened this classic flavor profile.

CONTESTANT:
Natalie
—
SEASON 2

# PORK CHOPS

## with APPLES, CARROTS, and MUSTARD SAUCE  serves 4

**Mustard Sauce**
2 cups pork stock
2 tablespoons unsalted butter
⅓ cup whole-grain mustard
½ teaspoon ground cumin
½ teaspoon ground coriander
Kosher salt and freshly ground
  black pepper

**Pork Chops**
4 double-cut bone-in pork chops
Kosher salt and freshly ground
  black pepper
¼ cup grapeseed oil
4 sprigs fresh rosemary
4 sprigs fresh thyme
4 garlic cloves

**Apples and Carrots**
2 tablespoons olive oil
1 tablespoon unsalted butter
2 bunches baby carrots
2 Granny Smith apples, peeled,
  cored, and cut into sixteenths
1 teaspoon ground cumin
2 tablespoons chopped fresh
  cilantro
Kosher salt and freshly ground
  black pepper

**1.** Make the mustard sauce: In a small saucepan, simmer the stock over medium-high heat until reduced to ½ cup, 10 to 15 minutes. Remove the pan from the heat and whisk in the butter, mustard, cumin, and coriander. Season with salt and pepper.

**2.** Make the pork chops: Preheat the oven to 350°F.

**3.** Generously season the pork chops with salt and pepper on all sides. In a large oven-safe sauté pan, heat the grapeseed oil over high heat. Sear the pork chops, flipping once, until browned on both sides, 3 to 4 minutes. Using tongs, lift up the chops and place 1 sprig of rosemary, 1 sprig of thyme, and 1 garlic clove underneath each chop. Transfer the pan to the oven and cook until the internal

temperature of the largest pork chop reaches 150°F, about 10 minutes. Transfer the chops to a plate and let rest for 10 minutes.

**4.** Meanwhile, make the apples and carrots: In a large sauté pan, heat the olive oil and butter over medium-high heat. Add the carrots and sauté, stirring occasionally, until slightly tender around the edges, about 3 minutes. Add the apples and cook, stirring, until both the carrots and apples have caramelized, 4 to 5 minutes. Add the cumin and cilantro and season with salt and pepper.

**5.** To serve, place a pork chop in the center of each of four plates. Arrange some apples and carrots next to each pork chop. Spoon the sauce over the pork.

When Jenna and Mia were paired together for this team challenge in Season 3, they discovered they were both half German, and decided to create this German-style dish. They mixed pork and chorizo together for a super-flavorful sausage, which judge Gordon Ramsay called "the best sausage of the year." They used a sausage stuffer to shape the meat into traditional pork casings, but don't worry if you don't have this piece of equipment at home; you can simply shape the meat mixture into patties. Try serving it with Roasted Potatoes (page 158) on the side for a hearty, satisfying meal!

CONTESTANTS:
Jenna
and Mia
—
SEASON 3

# PORK AND CHORIZO SAUSAGE
## with QUICK SAUERKRAUT  serves 4

**Quick Sauerkraut**
¼ cup olive oil
1 red onion, thinly sliced
½ small red cabbage, cored and thinly sliced
⅓ cup cider vinegar
¼ cup chicken stock

1½ tablespoons caraway seeds
Kosher salt and freshly ground black pepper

**Pork and Chorizo Sausage**
1 pound ground pork butt
¼ pound ground pork fat

¼ pound ground pork chorizo
¼ cup paprika
Kosher salt and freshly ground black pepper
4 pork casings, rinsed (optional)
2 tablespoons grapeseed oil

1. Make the quick sauerkraut: In a large sauté pan, heat the olive oil over high heat. Add the onion and cabbage and cook, stirring, until the cabbage wilts and browns, 5 to 7 minutes. Add the vinegar, stock, and caraway. Cover the pan and cook until the cabbage absorbs all the liquid, 15 to 20 minutes. Season with salt and pepper.

2. Make the sausage: Combine the pork butt, pork fat, chorizo, and paprika in a large bowl. Season generously with salt and pepper and mix thoroughly. Using a sausage stuffer, stuff the pork mixture into the casings, making sure there are no air pockets, and tie off the ends. (Alternatively, shape the meat mixture into 4 large or 8 small patties.) Place the sausages on a baking sheet and freeze for 30 minutes.

3. If using sausages stuffed in casings, place the sausages in a large pot of cold water and bring to a boil. Once the water boils, gently transfer the sausages to a paper towel–lined plate and let drain. (If using sausage patties, skip this step.)

4. In a large sauté pan, heat the grapeseed oil over medium-high heat. Add the boiled sausages or sausage patties and brown on all sides, turning to cook evenly, about 2 minutes per side. The internal temperature of the sausages should reach 135°F. Transfer to a plate and let rest for 10 minutes.

5. To serve, slice the stuffed sausages on the bias; keep the patties whole. Serve the sausages alongside the quick sauerkraut.

There are a lot of different parts to this recipe. Each one is worth cooking on its own, but all together they add up to something truly spectacular. This team of Juniors also made their own tortilla chips from scratch by first making corn tortillas and then frying them. At home you could fry store-bought corn tortillas until crisp, or just buy your favorite tortilla chips. Grilled Corn Succotash (page 170) would make a terrific side, and it was presented as part of this team's final dish.

Team Challenge
—
SEASON 4

# SPICE-CRUSTED PORK TENDERLOIN
## and BLACK BEAN CAKES  serves 4

**Avocado Mousse**
2 ripe Hass avocados, pitted and peeled
¼ cup sour cream
1 garlic clove, minced
Juice of 1 lime
1 tablespoon finely chopped fresh flat-leaf parsley
Kosher salt and freshly ground black pepper

**Tomatillo Sauce**
Kosher salt
7 tomatillos, husked and well rinsed
2 tablespoons grapeseed oil
1 garlic clove, minced

½ white onion, finely chopped
½ teaspoon cayenne
½ teaspoon ground cumin
2 ripe Hass avocados, pitted and peeled
¼ cup sour cream

**Black Bean Cakes**
¼ cup plus 2 tablespoons grapeseed oil
1 small yellow onion, finely chopped
1 garlic clove, minced
1 teaspoon ground cumin
1 teaspoon ground coriander
¼ teaspoon cayenne

2 (15-ounce) cans black beans, drained and rinsed
1 large egg, beaten
1 cup masa harina
Kosher salt and freshly ground black pepper

**Pork Tenderloin**
1 tablespoon cumin seeds
1 tablespoon coriander seeds
½ teaspoon cayenne
½ teaspoon ground cinnamon
1 (3-pound) pork tenderloin
Kosher salt and freshly ground black pepper

Corn tortilla chips, for serving

**1.** Make the avocado mousse: In a blender, combine the avocados, sour cream, garlic, and lime juice and blend until smooth. Stir in the parsley and season with salt and black pepper. Transfer to a small bowl, cover, and refrigerate until ready to serve.

**2.** Make the tomatillo sauce: Bring a medium pot of salted water to a boil. Add the tomatillos and cook until tender, 8 to 10 minutes. Drain.

**3.** In medium sauté pan, heat the grapeseed oil over medium-high heat. Add the garlic and onion and

*(Continued)*

cook, stirring, until lightly browned, 4 minutes. Stir in the cayenne, cumin, and a pinch of salt. Transfer the mixture to a blender. Add the avocados and cooked tomatillos and blend until smooth. Strain through a fine-mesh sieve into a bowl. Stir in the sour cream.

**4.** Make the black bean cakes: In a medium sauté pan, heat 2 tablespoons of the grapeseed oil over medium heat. Add the onion and garlic and cook, stirring, until lightly browned, 4 minutes. Stir in the cumin, coriander, and cayenne and cook for 1 minute. Transfer the mixture to a large bowl. Using a food processor, purée the beans until smooth, then add them to the onion mixture. Stir in the egg, ½ cup of the masa harina, and a pinch each of salt and black pepper. Shape into 8 patties (each about 1½ ounces) and dust with the remaining masa harina.

**5.** In a large nonstick pan, heat the remaining ¼ cup grapeseed oil over medium heat. Fry the black bean cakes until browned on both sides, 2 to 3 minutes per side. Transfer to a plate and sprinkle lightly with salt.

**6.** Cook the pork: Preheat the oven to 375°F.

**7.** In a small pan, toast the cumin and coriander (see Tip, page 57) over medium heat until aromatic, 2 to 3 minutes. In a spice grinder or coffee grinder, grind the toasted spices to a powder. Transfer to a small bowl and stir in the cayenne and cinnamon. Rub the spice mixture all over the pork tenderloin and season the meat generously with salt and black pepper.

**8.** Cook the pork tenderloin: Heat a grill or grill pan over high heat. Grill the pork until browned evenly on all sides, about 2 minutes per side. Transfer the pork to a baking sheet and roast until the internal temperature reaches 150°F, 6 to 8 minutes. Let rest at room temperature for 5 to 10 minutes, and then cut into thick slices.

**9.** To serve, place 2 black bean cakes on each of 4 plates. Arrange 3 or 4 slices of pork tenderloin beside the cakes and divide the tortilla chips among the plates. Spoon the avocado mousse onto the black bean cakes.

Avery felt fairly confident when she presented this dish, because she had cooked pork belly a few times before, but she did look completely surprised and delighted when judge Christina Tosi described it as "one of—if not the—most delicious dishes" she had ever tasted in the *MasterChef Junior* kitchen. Avery served this pork with Sweet Potato Purée (page 160), along with a fantastic, brightly colored garnish of pan-fried Brussels sprouts leaves and shaved beets.

# BRAISED PORK BELLY
## with APPLE CIDER GLAZE  serves 4

**Pork Belly**
2 pounds pork belly
Kosher salt and freshly ground
    black pepper
1 tablespoon Cajun seasoning mix
5 tablespoons grapeseed oil
1 yellow onion, quartered
2 carrots, chopped
2 celery stalks, chopped

4 garlic cloves, crushed
7 cups vegetable stock, warmed

**Apple Cider Glaze**
2 tablespoons grapeseed oil
1 cup finely chopped yellow onion
1 cup finely chopped celery
1 garlic clove, minced
2 cups vegetable stock

¼ cup cider vinegar
2½ tablespoons honey
2 tablespoons whole-grain
    mustard
2 tablespoons unsalted butter
Kosher salt and freshly ground
    black pepper

Celery leaves, for garnish

1. Cook the pork belly: Generously season the pork with salt, pepper, and the Cajun seasoning on all sides. Heat 2 tablespoons of the grapeseed oil in a pressure cooker over medium-high heat. Add the onion, carrots, celery, and garlic and cook, stirring, until softened, about 5 minutes. Add the stock and pork belly. Lock the lid of the pressure cooker and increase the heat to high. Once a steady stream of steam rises from the release valve, reduce the heat to medium-low and cook for 40 minutes.

2. Release the steam of the pressure cooker according to the manufacturer's instructions, and then open the lid. Transfer the pork belly to a plate.

3. In a large pan, heat the remaining 3 tablespoons grapeseed oil over high heat. Add the pork belly, skin-side down, and sear until the skin is crisped, about 4 minutes. Flip and cook the other side for

1 minute. Transfer the pork belly to a cutting board and cut it into 2-inch squares.

4. Make the apple cider glaze: In a medium pot, heat the grapeseed oil over medium-high heat. Add the onion, celery, and garlic and cook, stirring, until softened, 3 minutes. Pour in the stock and simmer until reduced by half, about 5 minutes. Strain through a fine-mesh sieve, discarding the solids, and return the sauce to the pot. Whisk in the vinegar, honey, and mustard. Reduce the heat to low and simmer until the sauce thickens slightly, 3 to 4 minutes. Remove the pot from the heat and whisk in the butter until melted and incorporated. Season with salt and pepper.

5. To serve, arrange the pork belly in the center of each of four plates. Drizzle the glaze over the meat and garnish with celery leaves.

Using cola to slowly braise pork is a brilliant way to achieve sweet caramel flavors, and is seen in plenty of Southern cookbooks. Here, Addison upped the ante by creating her own spice blend and serving these falling-off-the-bone-tender ribs and savory barbecue sauce with Potato Salad (page 159) and Summer Strawberry Salad (page 179) for a meal reminiscent of a fun backyard party. Parmesan Mashed Potatoes (page 156) or Grilled Corn Succotash (page 170) would also be delicious served alongside.

# COLA-BRAISED PORK RIBS
## with COLA BARBECUE SAUCE  serves 4

**Ribs**

3 pounds pork spare ribs

Kosher salt and freshly ground
   black pepper

3 (12-ounce) cans cola

2 quarts vegetable stock, warmed

1 yellow onion, quartered

3 celery stalks, chopped

2 carrots, chopped

5 juniper berries

2 cinnamon sticks

3 cardamom pods

5 allspice berries

5 garlic cloves

**Cola Barbecue Sauce**

2 (12-ounce) cans cola

2 teaspoons liquid smoke

5 garlic cloves

2 cardamom pods

1 cinnamon stick

5 juniper berries

5 allspice berries

1½ cups ketchup

2 tablespoons cider vinegar

Kosher salt and freshly ground
   black pepper

1. Make the ribs: Season the ribs generously with salt and pepper on all sides. Place the ribs, cola, stock, onion, celery, carrots, juniper, cinnamon, cardamom, allspice, and garlic in a pressure cooker. Lock the lid of the pressure cooker in place and cook on high heat. Once a steady stream of steam flows from the release valve, turn the heat down to medium-low and cook for 40 minutes.

2. Meanwhile, make the cola barbecue sauce: In a small saucepan, combine the cola, liquid smoke, garlic, cardamom pods, cinnamon stick, juniper berries, and allspice berries. Bring to a simmer over medium-low heat and cook until reduced to a syrupy consistency, 7 to 8 minutes. Strain, discarding the spices. Return the sauce to the saucepan, whisk in the ketchup and vinegar, and bring to a low simmer. Cook, stirring occasionally, until thickened, about 15 minutes. Season with salt and pepper.

3. When the ribs are done cooking, release the steam from the pressure cooker according to the manufacturer's instructions, and then open the lid and transfer the ribs to a large bowl. Glaze with the cola barbecue sauce, tossing to coat.

4. Heat a large grill pan over medium-high heat. Add the ribs and cook until charred, about 3 minutes. Let cool slightly before serving.

This dish is a special version of classic surf and turf. It's difficult to decide which half of the dish is best—the filet mignon, perfectly cooked and drizzled with balsamic reduction, or the whole lobster tail cloaked in a creamy beurre blanc. Luckily, you don't have to choose—you can enjoy them both, together! Plus, once you've mastered the two classic sauces in this dish, the balsamic reduction and the beurre blanc, you can try serving them with other dishes, like Roast Beef Tenderloin with Root Vegetable Hash (page 109), Beef Wellington (page 111), or even Venison Tenderloin with Braised Cabbage and Parsnip Purée (page 127).

CONTESTANT:
*Kaitlyn*
—
SEASON 4

# FILET MIGNON AND LOBSTER

## with BALSAMIC REDUCTION  serves 4

**Balsamic Reduction**
1½ cups balsamic vinegar
2 tablespoons sugar

**Lobster and Beurre Blanc**
Kosher salt
4 lobster tails
2 cups white wine
2 tablespoons fresh lemon juice
2 garlic cloves, minced

2 tablespoons finely chopped shallot
⅓ cup heavy cream
½ cup (1 stick) unsalted butter, cut into small pieces
Freshly ground white pepper

**Filet Mignon**
4 filet mignon steaks, about 6 ounces each
Kosher salt and freshly ground black pepper
3 tablespoons grapeseed oil
4 tablespoons (½ stick) unsalted butter, cut into small pieces
2 garlic cloves, crushed
2 sprigs fresh thyme
2 sprigs fresh rosemary

**1.** Make the balsamic reduction: Bring the balsamic vinegar and sugar to a simmer in a small saucepan set over medium-high heat. Cook until reduced to a syrupy consistency, about 20 minutes.

**2.** Make the lobster and beurre blanc: Bring a large pot of salted water to a boil. Prepare a bowl of ice water. Place a skewer lengthwise through the lobster tails to help maintain their shape as they cook. Add the lobster tails to the boiling water and cook for 4 minutes. Immediately transfer to the ice water.

When cool enough to handle, remove the shells, keeping the lobster meat intact as a single piece.

**3.** In a medium saucepan, combine the wine, lemon juice, garlic, and shallot. Bring to a simmer over medium-high heat and cook until reduced to about ½ cup, about 10 minutes. Whisk in the cream and cook for 1 minute. Remove the pan from the heat and whisk in the butter until melted. Season with salt and white pepper.

*(Continued)*

**4.** Cook the filet mignon: Generously season the steaks with salt and black pepper on all sides. In a cast-iron skillet, heat the grapeseed oil over medium-high heat. Sear until browned on both sides, 2 to 3 minutes per side. Add the butter, garlic, thyme, and rosemary to the pan and cook, using a spoon to baste the steak with the butter as it melts, until the internal temperature of the thickest part of each steak reaches 125°F, 4 to 5 minutes. Transfer the steaks to a plate and let rest for 5 minutes before slicing.

**5.** Just before serving, place the cooked lobster tails in the pan with the beurre blanc and warm over low heat for 3 to 4 minutes.

**6.** To serve, place the sliced filet mignon in the center of each of four plates. Arrange a lobster tail next to the steak and spoon a little of the beurre blanc sauce over the lobster. Drizzle the balsamic reduction over the steak.

## COOKING STEAK WITHOUT A GRILL

If you order a steak in a restaurant, the chef will use a searing-hot pan—not a grill—to cook it to perfection. Here's how you can replicate that technique at home: Generously season the steaks with salt and pepper on all sides. Heat 2 tablespoons grapeseed oil in a cast-iron skillet over medium-high heat. Once the oil is nice and hot, sear the steaks until browned on both sides, 2 to 3 minutes per side. Add 4 tablespoons (½ stick) unsalted butter, 2 crushed garlic cloves, and a few sprigs of fresh thyme to the pan. Cook for 4 to 5 minutes more, using a spoon to pour the melted butter over the steak. Transfer the steaks to a plate, but don't cut into them right away! Let them rest for at least 5 minutes, which will allow the juices to settle into the meat. You don't want to slice open that perfectly cooked steak too soon or you'll lose all the delicious juices!

This technique works well for all kinds of steaks, from boneless tenderloin cuts (filet mignon, châteaubriand, New York strip) to super-flavorful bone-in cuts (rib-eye, porterhouse). Depending on the size of the steak, it may need a little less or a little more cooking time. The best way to test for doneness is to measure the steak's internal temperature using a probe-style instant-read thermometer inserted into the thickest part of the meat and not touching any bone. The USDA recommends an internal temperature of 145°F for safely cooked beef (medium-well), but many people prefer their steaks a bit rarer. No matter your preferred doneness, this indoor technique is sure to leave your guests asking for more!

This roast beef tenderloin, served on a bed of root vegetable hash and topped with a buttery fried egg, would be wonderful for a holiday meal during the winter season. Troy chose to make the root vegetable hash with a mixture of sweet potatoes, parsnips, and turnips, although you could use any combination of root vegetables, including yams, rutabaga, and celery root. Try using different vegetables to see how it changes the dish!

CONTESTANT:
*Troy*
—
SEASON 1

# ROAST BEEF TENDERLOIN
## with ROOT VEGETABLE HASH  serves 4

2 sweet potatoes, peeled and finely diced

3 parsnips, peeled and finely diced

2 small turnips, peeled and finely diced

7 garlic cloves, minced

5 tablespoons extra-virgin olive oil

Kosher salt and freshly ground black pepper

2 tablespoons finely chopped fresh flat-leaf parsley, plus more for garnish

1½ pounds center-cut beef tenderloin, trussed by your butcher

4 tablespoons (½ stick) unsalted butter, cut into small pieces

1 sprig fresh thyme

1 shallot, minced

1 cup demi-glace (see page 40)

2 tablespoons grapeseed oil

4 large eggs

**1.** Preheat the oven to 400°F.

**2.** On a baking sheet, toss together the sweet potatoes, parsnips, turnips, 4 of the garlic cloves, and 3 tablespoons of the olive oil. Spread the vegetables in an even layer and sprinkle with salt and pepper. Roast until nicely caramelized, 30 to 40 minutes. Remove the pan from the oven and scatter the parsley over the top.

**3.** In a large sauté pan, heat the remaining 2 tablespoons olive oil over high heat. Generously season the beef with salt and pepper on all sides. Add the beef to the pan and sear, turning to brown evenly, until cooked almost to desired doneness, 7 to 10 minutes for medium-rare. (An instant-read thermometer inserted in the thickest part of the tenderloin should register 135°F for medium-rare.) Remove the pan from the heat. Add 2 tablespoons of the butter, 1 garlic clove, and the thyme to the pan and use a spoon to baste the meat with the butter as it melts. Transfer the beef to a plate and let rest for at least 10 minutes.

**4.** Meanwhile, make a pan sauce by returning the pan to the stovetop over medium heat. Add the shallot and the remaining 2 garlic cloves and cook, stirring, until translucent, 2 to 3 minutes. Pour in the demi-glace and bring to a simmer over medium-low heat. Remove the pan from the heat, add the remaining 2 tablespoons butter, and stir to incorporate. Season with salt and pepper.

(Continued)

**5.** In a large pan, heat the grapeseed oil over medium-high heat. Crack in the eggs, making sure they don't touch, and fry until the whites are set, about 5 minutes.

**6.** To serve, cut the roast beef tenderloin into thick slices. Place the root vegetable hash in the center of each of four large plates. Arrange a few slices of beef on top of the hash, spoon the pan sauce over the meat, and top with a fried egg and parsley.

## OUTSIDE THE STEAK-AND-POTATOES BOX

Steak and potatoes are a natural pairing, but there are so many ways to cook potatoes! If you're craving something creamy, try Sweet Potato Purée (page 160) or Parmesan Mashed Potatoes (page 156). On the other hand, crunchy shoestring fries (page 86) might be just the ticket instead. Roasted Potatoes (page 158), with their crisp, golden brown edges and tender interior, are also delicious. And instead of slicing the potatoes before roasting them, you could use whole tiny fingerling potatoes—and try using a stiff spatula or the back of a large spoon to smash the roasted fingerlings and sprinkle with finely chopped fresh chives before serving.

Another great and fancy way to serve steak is to drizzle it with a delicious sauce. There are a few classics to master: beurre blanc (page 105), balsamic reduction (page 105), hollandaise (page 52), and mushroom sauce (page 40). Did you know it's also easy to make a simple red wine sauce? Just simmer 1 (750-ml) bottle cabernet sauvignon until reduced to about 1 cup, about 30 minutes, and then whisk in 1 cup veal demi-glace and bring back to a simmer.

As we see in the *MasterChef Junior* kitchen, the sky's the limit when it comes to trying new things. Any of the dishes in the Sides & Salads chapter (page 154) could be a fun experiment. You never know what unexpected pairing might become your new favorite!

Cooking a classic beef Wellington means beginning with some serious preparation: a sautéed mixture of finely chopped mushrooms known as mushroom duxelles; a stack of savory chive crepes; and seared fillets of beef tenderloin. The crepes wrap around the mushrooms and beef, containing all their delicious juices, and then the whole thing gets wrapped in puff pastry, before finally baking until the crust is golden brown. It is quite the endeavor, but the result—perfectly medium-rare beef inside a flaky pastry crust—is so impressive that all your effort is well worth it in the end. For side dishes, try Parmesan Mashed Potatoes (page 156) and Balsamic-Glazed Carrots (page 161).

CONTESTANT:
*Afnan*
—
SEASON 5

# BEEF WELLINGTON

serves 4

### Chive Crepes
½ cup all-purpose flour
1 teaspoon sugar
Kosher salt
2 tablespoons unsalted butter, melted
½ cup milk, plus more as needed
1 egg
1 egg yolk
2 teaspoons chopped fresh chives
Nonstick cooking spray

### Mushroom Duxelles
1 pound button mushrooms
2 tablespoons extra-virgin olive oil
2 sprigs fresh thyme
Kosher salt

2 tablespoons grapeseed oil
4 Kobe beef tenderloin fillets, about 6 ounces each

2 tablespoons Dijon mustard
4 thin slices prosciutto
2 sheets frozen puff pastry, thawed
2 large eggs
Kosher salt
Mushroom Sauce (page 40), warmed

1. Make the chive crepes: In a medium bowl, combine the flour, sugar, and a pinch of salt.

2. In a separate medium bowl, combine the butter, milk, egg, and egg yolk. Using an immersion blender, blend the egg mixture into the flour mixture until smooth. Strain the batter and let it rest for 15 minutes (it will thicken as it sits, so you may need to thin it with more milk). Stir in the chives.

3. Heat a nonstick skillet over medium-low heat. Spray with nonstick cooking spray. Ladle just enough batter into the pan to coat the bottom of it; pour out any excess batter. Cook until the edges start to brown, 2 to 3 minutes. Gently flip the crepe and cook for 1 minute more. Transfer to a plate. Repeat with the remaining batter.

4. Make the mushroom duxelles: In a food processor, process the mushrooms until finely chopped.

5. In a large skillet, heat the olive oil over medium heat. Add the mushrooms and thyme and season with salt. Cook, stirring occasionally, until the liquid has evaporated and the mushrooms have browned,

*(Continued)*

15 minutes. Transfer to a paper towel–lined baking sheet and let cool.

**6.** In a large pan, heat the grapeseed oil over high heat. Add the beef fillets and hard sear, turning to brown evenly, until golden brown around the edges but still raw in the center, about 1 minute per side. Transfer the seared beef to a plate. Brush the mustard on all sides of the beef.

**7.** Place 1 chive crepe on a piece of plastic wrap. Lay 1 slice of prosciutto over the crepe. Spread about one-quarter of the mushroom duxelles in the middle of the crepe. Place 1 seared beef fillet on top of the mushrooms. Tightly roll the crepe up and over the beef, covering it completely and trimming any excess crepe. Wrap tightly in the plastic. Repeat to assemble the 3 other beef rolls. (There will be crepes left over; they're delicious for breakfast.) Refrigerate for at least 4 hours and up to overnight.

**8.** Cut each sheet of puff pastry in half and place each half on a piece of plastic wrap. In a small bowl, stir together the eggs and a pinch of salt. Brush egg wash across the puff pastry, reserving the extra egg wash. Unwrap the chilled beef rolls and place one in the middle of each piece of puff pastry. Tightly roll the puff pastry up and over the beef roll, covering it completely and trimming any excess pastry. Wrap each Wellington in plastic wrap and refrigerate for at least 4 hours and up to overnight.

**9.** Preheat the oven to 425°F.

**10.** Place the beef Wellingtons on a baking sheet and brush them with the reserved egg wash. Bake until golden brown, about 15 minutes for medium-rare beef, or an internal temperatue of 130°F. Remove from the oven and let rest for at least 5 minutes.

**11.** To serve, place 1 beef Wellington in the center of each of four plates. Serve the warm mushroom sauce alongside.

During a serious burger challenge, Gavin smartly wanted to be sure his burger stood out from the classic American varieties around him. By using ground beef and mild Italian sausage as the base and spreading the buns with a kalamata olive relish, he created these "Italian burgers." They had real international flair, especially when served alongside Burrata Salad (page 175). Feel free to play around with substituting different kinds of sausage or meat in place of the sausage and beef. For instance, if you like the flavor of lamb, you could turn these into "Mediterranean" burgers by using a mixture of ground lamb and beef and topping with feta instead of provolone.

CONTESTANT:
Gavin
—
SEASON 1

# ITALIAN BURGERS
## with KALAMATA OLIVE RELISH  serves 4

**Kalamata Olive Relish**
1 cup kalamata olives, pitted
1 cup mayonnaise
Lemon juice
Kosher salt and freshly ground
    black pepper

**Burgers**
1 pound mild Italian sausage,
    casings removed
½ pound ground beef
3 garlic cloves, minced
2 teaspoons dried Italian
    seasoning

1 red onion, thickly sliced
4 slices provolone cheese
4 brioche buns, sliced in half
2 vine-ripened tomatoes, sliced
Baby arugula

**1.** Make the olive relish: In a blender or food processor, combine the olives and mayonnaise and blend until smooth. Transfer to a small bowl and season with lemon juice, salt, and pepper.

**2.** Make the burgers: In a large bowl, combine the sausage, ground beef, garlic, and Italian seasoning. Form 4 patties that are slightly wider than the buns.

**3.** Heat a grill to medium or a grill pan over medium heat. Sear the patties, flipping once, until cooked through to your preference, about 4 minutes per side for medium, or an internal temperature of 130°F. While the burgers cook, sear the red onion as well, if you like grilled onions, 1 to 2 minutes per side. Just before the burgers are finished cooking, place the sliced cheese on top and let melt. Toast the buns.

**4.** To serve, spread olive relish on one side of a toasted bun. Add the meat, grilled onion, tomato, arugula, and finally the top bun. Repeat for the remaining burgers.

The tension was palpable when judge Gordon Ramsay began to slice the veal chop. "You should be expecting medium-rare," Alexander told the judges, nervously holding his breath and hoping the meat was cooked correctly. As Gordon finished slicing the veal and pulled his knife away, the chop opened up and everyone could see the beautiful pink color of perfectly cooked veal. All the judges agreed it was fantastic—both visually and in terms of taste. This amazing entrée crowned our first *MasterChef Junior* winner and set the tone for the seasons to come. These veal chops would also be delicious with Parmesan Mashed Potatoes (page 156).

# VEAL CHOPS WITH SUMMER SQUASH
## and FRIED SAGE LEAVES   serves 4

½ cup plus 2 tablespoons grapeseed oil, plus more as needed
8 fresh sage leaves
Kosher salt

4 veal rib chops, cut 1 inch thick (about 12 ounces each)
Freshly ground black pepper
4 tablespoons (½ stick) unsalted butter, cut into small pieces
8 garlic cloves, finely chopped

8 sprigs fresh thyme
1 cup mixed summer squash (such as baby zucchini, pattypan, and baby eight balls), sliced in half
1 tablespoon plus 1 teaspoon finely chopped shallot

**1.** In a small pan, heat ½ cup of the grapeseed oil over medium-high heat. Add the sage leaves and fry, turning once, until crisp, about 1 minute. Transfer to a paper towel–lined plate, season with salt, and let cool.

**2.** Generously season the veal chops with salt and pepper on both sides. In a large sauté pan, heat the remaining 2 tablespoons grapeseed oil over medium heat. Add 2 veal chops and sear, turning to brown evenly on both sides, until cooked almost to desired doneness, 4 to 6 minutes for medium-rare. Transfer the veal chops to a large plate. Repeat with the remaining veal chops, adding more oil to the pan if needed. Return all 4 veal chops to the pan, remove the pan from the heat, and add the butter, garlic, and thyme. Use a spoon to baste the veal with the butter as it melts. Transfer the veal to the plate and let rest for 5 minutes.

**3.** Meanwhile, return the pan to the stovetop over medium heat. Add the summer squash and shallot and cook, stirring occasionally, until the shallot is translucent and the squash is tender, about 2 minutes. Season with salt and pepper.

**4.** To serve, arrange the summer squash in the center of each of four plates, then place the veal chop on top. Garnish with the fried sage leaves.

"My favorite challenge was absolutely the finale, because, for me, it represented the culmination of everything I had learned in the other challenges." —Nathan

Nathan designed this dish to evoke the flavors and colors of springtime in France. Judge Gordon Ramsay complimented Nathan on his technique of turning white asparagus into a purée, which adds an important creamy element to the dish. Judge Joe Bastianich thought Nathan accomplished the feat of elevating lamb chops to another level, with flavors that are pure and unique to themselves. He summed up what everyone was thinking when he told Nathan, "This kind of dish is the future of cooking."

# LAMB CHOPS
## with WHITE ASPARAGUS PURÉE and MOREL MUSHROOMS  serves 4

2 pounds white asparagus
2 cups whole milk
2 cups heavy cream
Kosher salt
1 cup shelled fresh fava beans
2 tablespoons extra-virgin olive oil
2 cups morel mushrooms, cleaned
1 tablespoon unsalted butter

Freshly ground black pepper
2 cups panko bread crumbs
½ cup chopped fresh flat-leaf parsley
¼ cup chopped fresh chives
Zest of 2 lemons
2 racks of baby lamb chops, about 1½ pounds each, frenched (see page 38)

¼ cup grapeseed oil
¼ cup Dijon mustard
½ cup pistachio oil
¼ cup sherry vinegar
¼ cup chopped roasted unsalted pistachios
4 stalks green asparagus, thinly sliced lengthwise

1. In a medium pot, combine the white asparagus, milk, and cream. Generously season with salt. Bring to a simmer over medium-high heat and cook until the asparagus is tender, 20 to 25 minutes. Using tongs, transfer the asparagus to a blender, reserving the cooking liquid. Blend until smooth, adding cooking liquid a splash at a time if needed to thin the purée. Strain the purée through a fine-mesh sieve to make it very smooth.

2. Bring a large pot of salted water to a boil. Prepare a bowl of ice water. Add the shelled fava beans to the boiling water and cook until the skins are loose, about 3 minutes. Transfer to the ice water, let cool, and then remove and discard the fava bean skins.

3. In a large sauté pan, heat the olive oil over medium-high heat. Add the mushrooms and cook, stirring often, until tender, about 3 minutes. Add the peeled fava beans and butter and cook until completely tender, 2 to 3 minutes. Season with salt and pepper.

4. Preheat the oven to 375°F.

5. In a food processor, combine the bread crumbs, parsley, chives, and lemon zest. Pulse until well combined.

6. Generously season the lamb with salt and pepper on all sides. Heat the grapeseed oil in a large sauté pan set over high heat. Working in batches, add the

(Continued)

lamb to the pan and sear until golden brown on both sides, about 2 minutes per side. Transfer the lamb to a baking sheet. Spread an even layer of mustard over the meat part of the lamb (not the bones). Scatter the bread crumb mixture over the lamb, pressing it so it sticks to the mustard. Roast the lamb until the internal temperature reaches 125°F for medium-rare, 7 to 10 minutes. Remove from the oven and let rest for 10 minutes before slicing between the bones into individual chops.

**7.** Meanwhile, whisk together the pistachio oil and sherry vinegar. Season with salt and pepper. Add the pistachios and stir to combine.

**8.** To serve, spoon a heaping tablespoon of white asparagus purée in the center of each of four plates. Arrange the sautéed morels and favas to the side. Place 3 lamb chops on top of the purée. Drizzle the pistachio vinaigrette over the lamb and garnish with the green asparagus.

## NATHAN'S INSPIRATION TO COOK LAMB

As Nathan stepped into the *MasterChef Junior* kitchen for the last time, facing the challenge of the finale of Season 3, he drew inspiration from his family's Italian ancestry and made an incredibly delicious lamb chop dish. He felt inspired to cook such a delicate protein because, even though lamb isn't as popular as other kinds of meat here in the United States, he knew it is beloved in Italy, and he hoped he could showcase precisely why that is. His goal was to create a dish that reflected a very specific time of the year—the spring season. He served the lamb chops with white asparagus purée plus sautéed morel mushrooms and bright green fava beans. It will come as no surprise, then, to learn that Nathan's main inspirations when he cooks are "color and whatever is currently in season."

Thinking back on that finale dish, he says he was most nervous about cooking the lamb just right. What is Nathan's best tip for ensuring perfectly cooked lamb meat? "Sear the surface before roasting," he advises, "and check the internal temperature of the meat with a thermometer after every 2 to 3 minutes of roasting until it reaches 145°F." Give that technique a try and see if lamb becomes a little more popular for dinner at your own house!

Shepherd's pie, a traditional savory English dish, is essentially a casserole composed of a layer of seasoned ground meat topped with mashed potatoes. It's a comfort food, but not something you'd expect in a fine-dining establishment. However, Adaiah's version, which is deconstructed and then elegantly reassembled between layers of baked puff pastry, looks and tastes like a dish cooked by a professional chef. Or, in this case, an extraordinarily talented young home cook!

# DECONSTRUCTED SHEPHERD'S PIE

serves 4

### Lamb Filling

3 tablespoons grapeseed oil

¼ cup finely chopped red bell pepper

¼ cup finely chopped carrot

¼ cup finely chopped yellow onion

1 pound ground lamb

2 garlic cloves, minced

1 tablespoon onion powder

1 tablespoon finely chopped fresh rosemary

1 tablespoon finely chopped fresh thyme

2 tablespoons finely chopped fresh flat-leaf parsley

Kosher salt and freshly ground black pepper

### Pea and Pear Purée

Kosher salt

1 cup shelled fresh peas

1 Bartlett pear, cored and chopped

¼ cup sour cream

1 tablespoon finely chopped fresh thyme

1 tablespoon finely chopped fresh flat-leaf parsley

1 garlic clove, minced

Freshly ground black pepper

### Pepper Sauce

1 cup chopped red bell pepper

1 jalapeño, seeded and chopped

¼ cup shredded sharp cheddar cheese

¼ cup sour cream

1 tablespoon cream cheese

1 teaspoon ground turmeric

¼ teaspoon cayenne

1 teaspoon paprika

Kosher salt and freshly ground black pepper

All-purpose flour, for dusting

2 sheets frozen puff pastry, thawed

Parmesan Mashed Potatoes (page 156)

**1.** Make the lamb filling: Heat the grapeseed oil in a large sauté pan set over medium heat. Add the bell pepper, carrot, and onion and cook, stirring, until the onion is translucent, 2 to 3 minutes. Stir in the ground lamb, garlic, onion powder, rosemary, thyme, and parsley. Cook until the meat is evenly browned and cooked through, 6 to 7 minutes. Season with salt and black pepper and keep warm.

**2.** Make the pea and pear purée: Bring a large pot of salted water to a boil. Add the peas and cook

*(Continued)*

until tender, 4 to 5 minutes. Strain. Put the peas in a blender and add the pear, sour cream, and ¼ cup water. Blend until smooth. Transfer to a bowl and stir in the thyme, parsley, and garlic. Season with salt and black pepper.

**3.** Make the pepper sauce: Using a blender, purée the bell pepper, jalapeño, cheddar, sour cream, and cream cheese until smooth. Transfer to a bowl and stir in the turmeric, cayenne, and paprika. Season with salt and black pepper.

**4.** Preheat the oven to 350°F. Line two baking sheets with parchment paper.

**5.** On a lightly floured surface, roll out the puff pastry sheets to flatten them and remove the crease.

Using a large round cutter, cut out six 3-inch rounds from each sheet. Place the rounds on the prepared baking sheets and cover with a nonstick baking mat or another piece of parchment paper. Place an additional baking sheet on top as a weight. Bake until the puff pastry is golden, 12 to 15 minutes.

**6.** To serve, place 1 puff pastry round in the center of each of four plates. Spread 1 heaping tablespoon of mashed potatoes over the pastry, and then spread 1 heaping tablespoon of ground lamb over the potatoes. Place another puff pastry round on top. Repeat to layer more mashed potatoes and ground lamb, topping the stack with a third puff pastry round. Serve the pea and pear purée and the pepper sauce on the side.

When you buy lamb racks for this recipe, you can ask the butcher to "french" the racks, meaning remove the small amount of meat attached to the top of each bone. Or, if you want to show off your own knife skills, you could french the lamb racks yourself, following the instructions on page 38. Spaetzle are tiny fresh egg noodles made by pressing batter through the small holes of a spaetzle maker. If you don't have this specific kitchen tool, use a regular colander instead.

# HERB-CRUSTED LAMB
## with SPAETZLE and MINT SAUCE    serves 4

**Mint Sauce**
¼ cup fresh mint leaves, finely chopped
1 tablespoon confectioners' sugar
3 tablespoons white wine vinegar
¼ teaspoon kosher salt

**Spaetzle**
Kosher salt
2 cups all-purpose flour
7 large egg yolks
¼ cup whole milk
2 tablespoons unsalted butter
Freshly ground black pepper

**Herb-Crusted Lamb**
3 tablespoons honey
6 tablespoons (¾ stick) unsalted butter, at room temperature
4 garlic cloves, minced
4 oil-packed or salt-packed anchovy fillets, rinsed and finely chopped
1½ cups panko bread crumbs
3 tablespoons finely chopped fresh flat-leaf parsley

1 tablespoon finely chopped fresh rosemary
1 tablespoon kosher salt, plus more for seasoning
1 teaspoon freshly ground black pepper, plus more for seasoning
3 tablespoons grapeseed oil
2 racks of lamb, frenched
¼ cup Dijon mustard

Pomegranate seeds, for garnish

**1.** Make the mint sauce: In a small saucepan set over medium heat, combine the mint, sugar, vinegar, salt, and 3 tablespoons water and bring to a simmer. Cook, stirring, until thick and creamy, 8 to 10 minutes.

**2.** Make the spaetzle: Bring a large pot of salted water to a boil. Prepare a bowl of ice water. In a large bowl, whisk together the flour, egg yolks, and milk. Using a spaetzle cutter, scrape the dough through the holes directly into the boiling water. (Alternatively, transfer the spaetzle batter to a colander and use a rubber spatula to scrape along

the bottom and sides of the colander, forcing the batter through the holes of the colander and letting the spaetzle drop directly into the boiling water.) Cook the spaetzle until it floats, about 3 minutes. Use a slotted spoon to transfer the spaetzle to the ice bath. Let cool for 1 minute and then drain.

**3.** In a large sauté pan, melt the butter over medium-high heat. Add the spaetzle and cook, stirring, until browned, about 3 minutes. Season with salt and pepper.

**4.** Cook the herb-crusted lamb: Preheat the oven to 350°F.

**5.** In a small bowl, stir together the honey, butter, garlic, anchovies, bread crumbs, parsley, rosemary, salt, and pepper.

**6.** In a large sauté pan, heat the grapeseed oil over high heat. Generously season the lamb with salt and pepper on all sides. Place 1 rack of lamb into the pan and sear until caramelized, about 5 minutes per side. Transfer the lamb to a plate and brush with about half of the mustard. Repeat with the remaining rack of lamb.

**7.** Press the bread crumb mixture onto the lamb racks to create a crust. Place the lamb racks on a baking sheet and roast until golden brown and the internal temperature reaches 125°F to 130°F, 10 to 15 minutes. Remove from the oven and let rest at least 10 minutes before slicing each rack between the bones.

**8.** To serve, spoon the spaetzle in the center of each of four plates. Place the herb-crusted lamb on top of the spaetzle and spoon mint sauce over the lamb. Garnish with pomegranate seeds.

Cooking venison is a real accomplishment in and of itself, since its gamy flavor can be overpowering. Amaya, Zac, and Avery did an excellent job with this dish, as the sautéed chanterelle mushrooms tossed in a pan with boiled gnocchi is a perfect partner. To sauté chanterelles or any other type of mushroom, you can use the same technique as in the recipe for Sautéed Broccolini (page 168). If you'd like to make homemade gnocchi as well, see page 133 for a recipe for regular gnocchi or page 135 for a version made with purple potatoes.

Team Challenge — SEASON 4

# VENISON TENDERLOIN
## with BRAISED CABBAGE and PARSNIP PURÉE serves 4

**Braised Cabbage**
2 tablespoons grapeseed oil
¼ cup diced pancetta
1 tablespoon minced garlic
1 tablespoon finely chopped shallot
½ cup white wine
1 small savoy cabbage, cored and thinly sliced
3 cups chicken stock
Kosher salt and freshly ground black pepper

**Parsnip Purée**
1 pound parsnips, peeled and thinly sliced
2 tablespoons unsalted butter
1 cup whole milk
Kosher salt

**Venison Tenderloin**
4 venison tenderloins (each about 8 ounces)
Kosher salt and freshly ground black pepper
3 tablespoons grapeseed oil
½ cup (1 stick) unsalted butter, cut into small pieces
4 garlic cloves, crushed
3 sprigs fresh thyme

**1.** Make the braised cabbage: In a large sauté pan, heat the grapeseed oil over medium-high heat. Add the pancetta and cook, stirring, until browned, 3 minutes. Transfer the pancetta to a plate, leaving the fat in the pan. Add the garlic and shallot to the pan and cook, stirring, for 1 minute. Pour in the wine and use a wooden spoon to scrape up any brown bits on the bottom of the pan. Add the cabbage and stock and season with salt and pepper. Reduce the heat to low and cook, stirring occasionally, until the cabbage is tender, about 4 minutes. Remove the pan from the heat and stir in the cooked pancetta. Keep warm.

**2.** Make the parsnip purée: In a medium saucepan, combine the parsnips, butter, and milk. Bring to a boil over high heat. Reduce the heat to low, cover the pan, and cook until the parsnips are very soft, 12 to 15 minutes. Drain the parsnips in a colander, reserving the liquid. Purée the parsnips in a blender until smooth, adding cooking liquid as needed to achieve your desired consistency. Season the purée with salt.

**3.** Cook the venison tenderloin: Preheat the oven to 375°F.

**4.** Generously season the venison loins with salt and pepper. In a large, oven-safe pan, heat the grapeseed oil over medium-high heat. Add the venison and cook until browned on all sides, about 1 minute on each side. Add the butter, garlic, and thyme and

*(Continued)*

spoon the melted butter over the venison. Transfer the pan to the oven and continue to roast until the internal temperature of the tenderloins reaches 145°F for medium-rare, 5 to 6 minutes. Transfer the venison to a cutting board and let rest for 5 to 8 minutes before slicing.

**5.** To serve, spoon braised cabbage and parsnip purée in the center of each of four plates. Top with the venison tenderloin.

## CHALLENGES OF COOKING VENISON

Venison is one of the most popular game meats and can be truly delicious, but there are a few important tips and tricks to keep in mind when preparing and cooking it. It's obviously not the same as corn-fed beef, which has much more fat. Wild deer graze on a range of plants and berries, including acorns, grasses, and aromatic herbs, and the animals are quite lean. Their meat often has a strong flavor, so cooking it properly is key.

The most important tip is to make sure not to overcook it. Tender cuts of venison are best served medium-rare or rare. Use an instant-read kitchen thermometer to check the internal temperature of the meat as it cooks. (Stop cooking it when the thermometer reaches 130°F for rare and 140°F to 145°F for medium-rare.) To boost natural fats and add an even richer, terrific flavor, baste the venison with melted butter while it cooks, as we do in the venison tenderloin recipe on page 127. Lastly (and this is actually true for all meat), let the cooked venison rest for at least 5 minutes before slicing it. After such a perfect preparation, you want to be sure to give the juices a chance to settle so they don't run out when you cut it!

A tantalizing mixture of spices gives this goat curry a real depth of flavor and also stands up to the meatiness of the goat. If you are short on time, you can skip the frying of the shallots and instead pick up a bag of fried shallots at an Asian market or a specialty foods store.

# GOAT CURRY
## with CILANTRO RICE and CRISPY SHALLOTS   serves 4

Vegetable oil, for frying
2 shallots, thinly sliced
1 cup all-purpose flour
Kosher salt
2 pounds goat meat, cut into 1-inch cubes
Freshly ground black pepper

3 tablespoons grapeseed oil
1 yellow onion, chopped
1 large carrot, chopped
6 tablespoons tomato paste
4 cups chicken stock
2 tablespoons vadouvan spice blend (see Tip, page 67)

Zest and juice of 2 limes
1 serrano chile, stemmed and seeded
2 cups long-grain rice
1 tablespoon unsalted butter
½ cup chopped fresh cilantro
Micro cilantro, for garnish

1. In a heavy pot, heat at least 1 inch of vegetable oil to 350°F. Dredge the shallots in ½ cup of the flour, shaking off the excess, and carefully place them in the hot oil. Fry until golden, 3 to 4 minutes. Transfer to a paper towel–lined plate, season with salt, and let cool.

2. Generously season the goat meat with salt and pepper on all sides. Heat the grapeseed oil in a pressure cooker set to the high setting. Add the goat meat and cook, turning to evenly sear all sides, until browned, about 3 minutes per side. Transfer the meat to a plate. Add the onion and carrot and cook, stirring, until the onion is translucent, 1 minute. Return the goat meat to the pressure cooker and add the tomato paste, chicken stock, vadouvan, the remaining ½ cup flour, and the lime zest and juice. Cut off the tip of the serrano chile and add it to the pressure cooker. Cover and cook over medium heat

for 15 minutes, until you can hear a steam hissing sound. Turn the pressure cooker off and let cool with the lid on for about 5 minutes to reduce steam pressure. Cook over medium heat for 15 minutes more, then remove the lid and continue cooking for 10 minutes, or until the sauce thickens.

3. Meanwhile, in a large saucepan set over medium-high heat, combine the rice, butter, 1 teaspoon salt, and 4 cups water. Bring to a boil and cook, uncovered, until you see holes forming on the surface, about 15 minutes. Reduce the heat to the lowest setting, cover the pan, and cook for 20 minutes. Remove the pan from the heat, add the cilantro, and use a fork to fluff the rice.

4. To serve, place about 1 cup of cilantro rice in the center of each plate or shallow bowl. Spoon some of the goat curry over the rice. Garnish with the crispy shallots and micro cilantro.

PASTA

Gnocchi are delicious, plump dumplings that can be served with all kinds of pasta sauces. They're often made with potatoes, which gives them a satisfying, gooey texture. To create the grooves that distinguish gnocchi from other shapes of pasta, you don't need any special tools (although there is a tool that exists for just this purpose). You can simply roll the gnocchi across the tines of a regular fork.

# GNOCCHI
## with BROWN BUTTER–SAGE SAUCE and TOMATOES serves 4

Kosher salt

2 russet potatoes, peeled and cut into 1-inch cubes

1½ cups all-purpose flour, plus more for dusting

1 large egg

5 tablespoons unsalted butter

1 cup vine-ripened cherry tomatoes

1 garlic clove, minced

2 tablespoons chopped fresh sage

2 tablespoons chopped fresh oregano

**1.** Bring a pot of generously salted water to a boil. Add the potatoes and boil until tender, about 15 minutes. Drain and let cool. Using a ricer or a potato masher, mash the potatoes. Stir in the flour and egg. Transfer the potato mixture to a floured surface and knead into a smooth ball. Wrap the dough in plastic wrap and let rest at room temperature for 5 minutes.

**2.** Cut the ball of dough into 4 pieces. On a floured work surface, roll each piece into a log about ¾ inch thick. Cut crosswise into ¾- to 1-inch-long pieces. Press and roll each piece across the tines of a fork to create ridges on one side. Place the rolled gnocchi on a floured baking sheet as you go.

**3.** Bring another pot of generously salted water to a boil. Add the gnocchi and cook until they rise to the surface, 3 to 5 minutes.

**4.** Meanwhile, in a large sauté pan, melt the butter over medium-high heat. Add the tomatoes, garlic, and herbs. Cook, stirring often, until the butter browns and tomatoes blister, 6 minutes. Using a slotted spoon, transfer the cooked gnocchi to the pan. Toss to coat. Season with salt. Divide the gnocchi among four plates and serve immediately.

"Keep a flavor journal and experiment with layering flavors, and of course learn as much as you can about food. Trying everything is key to finding elusive flavors you might need later." —Logan

Even the garnishes on this dish are impressive: grilled slices of fennel bulb, salty preserved lemon rind, green olives, and more! Feel free to pick and choose the garnishes you'd like to use—they are all optional. The real heart of this dish is the amazing tomato-saffron broth, plus the gorgeous deeply colored gnocchi made with purple potatoes. Pan-seared snapper, known for its bright pinkish-red skin, adds another nice pop of color, but you could substitute any fresh fish. Saffron is the most expensive spice in the world and is known for its rich, earthy flavor, which makes this dish so special. If you don't want to use the full amount of saffron called for in the recipe, you can use just a pinch or try flavoring the broth with another seasoning you like.

# GNOCCHI AND SNAPPER
## in TOMATO-SAFFRON BROTH serves 4

1 pound purple potatoes

1 large egg

½ cup all-purpose flour, plus more for dusting

Kosher salt and freshly ground black pepper

¼ cup plus 3 tablespoons extra-virgin olive oil

½ cup diced Spanish (cured) chorizo

1 tablespoon minced garlic

2 tablespoons minced shallot

5 sprigs fresh oregano

10 sprigs fresh thyme

2 cups white wine

2 teaspoons saffron

4 cups chicken stock

3 cups tomato sauce

3 tablespoons unsalted butter

4 skin-on snapper fillets, about 5 ounces each

**Optional Garnishes**

1 large fennel bulb, sliced and grilled

1 cup cherry tomatoes, quartered

½ cup sliced green olives

1 tablespoon finely chopped preserved lemon rind

¼ cup fennel fronds

1. Preheat the oven to 350°F.

2. Poke a few holes in the potatoes with a fork, wrap each in aluminum foil, and place them all on a baking sheet. Bake until tender, about 40 minutes. Remove the foil, let cool slightly, and peel off and discard the potato skins. Using a ricer or a potato masher, mash the potatoes. Stir in the egg and flour. Transfer the potato mixture to a floured surface and knead into a smooth ball. Wrap the dough in plastic and let rest at room temperature for 5 minutes.

3. Cut the ball of dough into 2 pieces. On a floured surface, roll each piece into a log about ½ inch thick. Cut crosswise into ¾-inch-long pieces. Press and roll each piece across a gnocchi board or the tines of a fork to create ridges on one side. Place the rolled gnocchi on a floured baking sheet as you go.

4. Bring a pot of generously salted water to a boil. Add the rolled gnocchi and cook until they rise to the surface, 3 to 5 minutes.

*(Continued)*

**5.** Meanwhile, in a large pan, heat 2 tablespoons of the olive oil over medium heat. Using a slotted spoon, transfer the cooked gnocchi directly to the pan. Cook, stirring occasionally, until lightly browned on both sides, about 5 minutes.

**6.** In a large pot, heat ¼ cup of the oil over medium heat. Add the chorizo and cook, stirring, until browned, 3 to 5 minutes. Add the garlic, shallot, oregano, and thyme and cook, stirring, for 1 to 2 minutes. Pour in the wine and simmer until reduced by about one-third, about 3 minutes. Add the saffron, stock, and tomato sauce. Reduce the heat to low and simmer until the broth thickens slightly, about 20 minutes. Season with salt and pepper. Remove and discard the herb sprigs. Remove the broth from the heat, and stir in the butter until melted.

**7.** In a large pan, heat the remaining 1 tablespoon oil over medium heat. Add the snapper, skin-side down, and cook until browned on the first side, about 4 minutes. Flip and cook until the snapper is just barely cooked through, about 2 minutes.

**8.** To serve, spoon about 6 tablespoons of tomato-saffron broth into each of four serving bowls. Place grilled fennel, if using, in the center of each bowl and top with 1 fillet of snapper, skin-side up. Arrange 5 gnocchi in the broth around the fish. If using, scatter cherry tomatoes, green olives, preserved lemon, and fennel fronds over the snapper.

If you are looking for a delicious and comforting pasta dish, this one hits all the right marks! It's creamy and rich, with a thick sauce that clings to the fresh noodles. The sauce itself is worth making, even if you don't prepare the noodles from scratch. Try serving the sauce over any of your favorite noodle shapes, from short farfalle to long, ribbonlike fettuccine.

# PAPPARDELLE
## with BACON CREAM SAUCE  serves 4

Fresh Pasta Dough (page 140)
Semolina, plus more for dusting
½ cup chopped bacon

2 tablespoons unsalted butter
2 cups heavy cream
1 teaspoon freshly ground black pepper

Kosher salt
Extra-virgin olive oil, for tossing
¼ cup grated Parmesan cheese

1. Roll the pasta dough through a pasta machine, gradually making the dough thinner and thinner, until it is as thin as possible. Cut the dough into ¾-inch-wide strips. Place the pasta strips on a semolina-floured baking sheet and cover with a kitchen towel until you are ready to cook the pasta.

2. In a medium sauté pan, cook the bacon over medium-high heat, stirring, until lightly browned, 5 to 7 minutes. Transfer to a paper towel–lined plate and let cool.

3. In a small saucepan, melt the butter over medium heat. Whisk in 2 tablespoons of the semolina and cook, whisking, until smooth, 1 minute. Whisk in the cream and simmer until thickened, 4 to 5 minutes. Remove the pan from the heat and stir in the pepper and cooked bacon.

4. Bring a large pot of salted water to a boil. Cook the pasta until al dente, 2 to 3 minutes. Drain and toss with olive oil. Toss the cooked pasta with the bacon cream sauce. To serve, divide the pappardelle among four plates and sprinkle some Parmesan over each.

## MAKING PASTA BY HAND

In the *MasterChef Junior* kitchen, most of the contestants use their hands to make fresh pasta directly on a flat work surface, just like Italian grandmothers have done for generations. They don't even use a bowl to mix the dough! Sometimes the contestants will change up the recipe, adding only whole eggs or incorporating additional egg yolks. Have you ever eaten pasta that is bright orange-yellow in color and super rich in flavor? Generally, the more yolks used, the richer the pasta dough.

Because they have access to state-of-the-art kitchen equipment, Juniors usually use a countertop pasta roller to roll the dough out into thin sheets. But you don't need fancy tools to make pasta at home! If you don't happen to have a roller, you can use a rolling pin. It takes a little more elbow grease, but it's easy enough to roll out the dough into thin pieces, making sure to keep the thickness even throughout so that the pasta cooks evenly.

Here's a recipe that'll work for all the recipes in this chapter (except for the risotto and gnocchi).

# Fresh Pasta Dough makes 1 pound

4 cups all-purpose
  flour
4 large eggs

9 large egg yolks
1 tablespoon olive oil,
  plus more for tossing

Kosher salt

**1.** Pile the flour on a clean, dry surface and make a well in the center, like a volcano. Crack the eggs and egg yolks into the well. Add the olive oil and a pinch of salt. Using a fork, slowly stir the eggs to break up the yolks, scraping gently along the sides and pulling flour into the well. Continue stirring until most of the flour has been incorporated, and then use your hands to knead the mixture into a smooth dough. If the dough is dry and flaky and you can't mix in all the flour, add warm water, 1 tablespoon at a time, until the dough feels elastic. Cover with plastic wrap or a clean kitchen towel and set aside to rest for at least 20 minutes and up to 1 hour.

**2.** Roll and cut the pasta according to the recipe or your desired shape. Boil the fresh pasta in salted water, toss with sauce, and serve. *Buon appetito!*

"One of my favorite memories from the show was when I had the advantage of not having to cook in a challenge. Not only was it relaxing, but I had an opportunity to watch the other contestants cook, which helped me learn new skills since I didn't have to focus on cooking." —Nathan

Jimmy created this sauce to taste like a traditional vodka sauce, but there's no vodka in it. Instead, he just used a bit more cheese and cream. Judge Gordon Ramsay called this dish "absolutely delicious," praising both the richness of the sauce and the texture of the fresh pasta. You can certainly add a splash of vodka, if you want, to give the sauce something extra.

# PAPPARDELLE
## with "VODKA/NO VODKA" SAUSAGE SAUCE  serves 4

Fresh Pasta Dough (page 140)
Semolina, for dusting
3 tablespoons extra-virgin olive oil, plus more for drizzling
3 garlic cloves, minced
1 (28-ounce) can whole peeled tomatoes, crushed by hand

2 tablespoons chopped fresh basil, plus whole basil leaves for serving
1 tablespoon chopped fresh parsley
1 tablespoon chopped fresh oregano

2 hot Italian sausages, casing removed
½ cup heavy cream
¼ cup grated Parmesan cheese, plus more for serving
Kosher salt and freshly ground black pepper

**1.** Roll the pasta dough through a pasta machine, gradually making the dough thinner and thinner, until it is as thin as possible. Cut the dough into ¾-inch-wide strips. Place the pasta strips on a semolina-floured baking sheet and cover with a kitchen towel until you are ready to cook the pasta.

**2.** In a large sauté pan, heat the olive oil over medium heat. Add the garlic and cook, stirring, until softened, about 1 minute. Stir in the crushed tomatoes, basil, parsley, and oregano. Use a wooden spoon to crush and break up the tomatoes. Bring to a simmer and cook, stirring occasionally, until slightly thickened, 15 to 20 minutes.

**3.** In a separate pan, brown the sausage over medium heat, stirring to break up the meat into small pieces, 7 to 10 minutes. Transfer the sausage to the pan with the tomato sauce. Add the cream and Parmesan. Season with salt and pepper. Keep warm.

**4.** Bring a large pot of salted water to a boil. Cook the pasta until al dente, 2 to 3 minutes. Drain and toss with a drizzle of olive oil to prevent sticking. Transfer the cooked pasta to the pan of "vodka/no vodka" sauce and stir well to coat. Serve each plate of pasta topped with grated Parmesan and fresh basil leaves.

Judge Graham Elliot was incredibly impressed by the technique Ryan Kate used to cut the fresh basil leaves for this pasta. He told her that mastering a chiffonade—tightly rolling whole herb leaves and then thinly slicing them into ribbons—was a skill most cooks don't learn until culinary school. But Ryan Kate (at the young age of eleven!) had already practiced this skill numerous times and had the technique down.

CONTESTANT:
Ryan Kate
—
SEASON 3

# PAPPARDELLE
## with TOMATO BASIL MUSHROOM SAUCE  serves 4

Fresh Pasta Dough (page 140)
Semolina, for dusting
3 tablespoons extra-virgin olive oil, plus more for drizzling

2 garlic cloves, minced
1 shallot, finely chopped
6 tomatoes, quartered
10 button mushrooms, chopped

Kosher salt and freshly ground black pepper
9 fresh basil leaves, thinly sliced, plus 4 whole leaves for garnish

**1.** Roll the pasta dough through a pasta machine, gradually making the dough thinner and thinner, until it is as thin as possible. Cut the dough into ¾-inch-wide strips. Place the pasta strips on a semolina-floured baking sheet and cover with a kitchen towel until you are ready to cook the pasta.

**2.** In a large sauté pan, heat the olive oil over medium heat. Add the garlic and shallot and cook, stirring, until soft, about 4 minutes. Add the tomatoes and mushrooms and cook, stirring

occasionally, until the tomatoes soften and release their juices, 5 minutes. Remove the pan from the heat, season the sauce with salt and pepper, and fold in the sliced basil.

**3.** Bring a large pot of salted water to a boil. Cook the pasta until al dente, 2 to 3 minutes. Drain and toss with a drizzle of olive oil to prevent sticking. Transfer the cooked noodles to the pan of tomato basil mushroom sauce and stir well to coat. Serve each plate of pasta garnished with a fresh basil leaf.

The first tortellini Gavin ever tasted was from a deli near his San Francisco home, and it was love at first bite. He wanted to see if he could cook them in his own kitchen, so he started experimenting. When Judge Joe Bastianich took a bite of the beef-filled version Gavin made, he was so impressed that he said, "Are you sure you didn't learn to make tortellini in Italy?" Try your hand with these, and see if your guests can guess where you learned them!

CONTESTANT:
Gavin
—
SEASON 1

# BEEF TORTELLINI
## with SAGE-BUTTER SAUCE  *serves 4 to 6*

Fresh Pasta Dough (page 140)
All-purpose flour, for dusting
½ pound ground beef
2 large eggs

½ cup grated pecorino cheese, plus more for serving
Freshly ground black pepper
Kosher salt

6 tablespoons (¾ stick) unsalted butter
12 fresh sage leaves, finely chopped

**1.** Roll the pasta dough through a pasta roller, gradually making the dough thinner and thinner until it is your desired thickness. Cut into 1-inch-wide strips. Place the pasta strips on a floured baking sheet and cover with a kitchen towel until you are ready to fill the tortellini.

**2.** In a large skillet, cook the beef over medium heat until browned through, about 7 minutes. Transfer to a food processor, add the eggs and ½ cup of the grated pecorino, and process to combine. Season with pepper. Let cool to room temperature.

**3.** On a floured work surface, uncover the pasta strips and spread them out flat. Cut the dough into 1-inch squares. Place about 1 teaspoon of the filling in the center of each square. Brush the edges with water, and then fold into a triangle, pressing firmly to seal. Pinch the two farthest points of the triangle together to form a tortellini shape. Cover the filled pasta while you make the remaining tortellini.

**4.** Bring a large pot of salted water to a boil. Cook the tortellini until al dente, 3 to 4 minutes.

**5.** Meanwhile, in a large skillet, melt the butter over medium-low heat. Stir in the sage and cook until crisp, 3 minutes. Using a slotted spoon, transfer the cooked tortellini to the skillet and toss to coat evenly in the sage-butter sauce. Serve topped with grated cheese.

You can cut sheets of fresh pasta dough into noodles of any width, from broad ribbons of pappardelle to thin strands of spaghetti. Troy called his version pappardelle, but cut the noodles slightly thinner than this traditional wide noodle to make fettuccine. If you're buying fresh noodles, either would work. If you're making them yourself, feel free to cut the pasta dough as wide as you'd like. You're the cook in charge, so the decision is entirely up to you, and that's what makes it fun!

CONTESTANT:
*Troy*
—
SEASON 1

# FETTUCCINE
## with SHELLFISH in WHITE WINE SAUCE   serves 4

Fresh Pasta Dough (page 140)
Semolina, for dusting
3 tablespoons extra-virgin olive oil, plus more for drizzling
8 jumbo scallops
Kosher salt and freshly ground black pepper

12 large shrimp, peeled and deveined
4 tablespoons (½ stick) unsalted butter
6 garlic cloves, minced
1 bunch asparagus, trimmed
1 cup mixed red and yellow cherry tomatoes, halved

1 cup white wine (nonalcoholic wine is fine to use)
1 pound baby spinach, chopped
Grated Parmesan cheese, for serving

**1.** Roll the pasta dough through a pasta machine, gradually making the dough thinner and thinner, until it is as thin as possible. Cut the dough into ¼-inch-wide strips. Place the pasta strips on a semolina-floured baking sheet and cover with a kitchen towel until you are ready to cook the pasta.

**2.** In a large pan, heat 2 tablespoons of the olive oil over high heat. Season the scallops with salt and pepper on both sides and put them into the hot pan. Sear each side for 90 seconds. Transfer the scallops to a plate. Add the remaining 1 tablespoon olive oil to the pan. Add the shrimp and cook, flipping once, until cooked through, about 3 minutes. Transfer to the plate with the scallops.

**3.** Melt 2 tablespoons of the butter in the pan. Add the garlic and asparagus and cook, stirring occasionally, until tender, about 3 minutes. Stir in the tomatoes and white wine. Simmer until the liquid reduces by half, 2 to 3 minutes. Remove the pan from the heat, add the remaining 2 tablespoons butter and the spinach, and stir until the butter melts and the spinach wilts. Season with salt and pepper. Return the shellfish to the sauce.

**4.** Bring a large pot of salted water to a boil. Cook the pasta until al dente, 4 to 5 minutes. Drain and toss with a drizzle of olive oil to prevent sticking. Add the cooked pasta to the pan of white wine sauce and stir well to coat. Serve topped with Parmesan.

Andrew made this fresh pasta with "00" flour instead of the more common all-purpose flour. Throughout Italy and in other parts of Europe, many cooks will often use "00" (or *doppio zero*) flour, which is very finely ground, when making fresh pasta because it gives the noodles a distinct texture. Using all-purpose flour instead will work fine, but it is definitely worth making fresh pasta with double-zero flour at least once to see if you like it. You can get it at specialty grocery stores or online.

# BEEF CHEEK AGNOLOTTI

serves 4

2 cups "00" flour

2 large eggs, plus 1 egg, beaten, for egg wash

5 large egg yolks

3 tablespoons extra-virgin olive oil

Kosher salt

Semolina, for dusting

1 pound beef cheeks, cleaned

Freshly ground black pepper

1 onion, chopped

3 garlic cloves, smashed

1 tablespoon anchovy paste

1 teaspoon crushed red pepper flakes

4 cups beef stock

¼ cup grated Grana Padano cheese, plus more for garnish

2 tablespoons unsalted butter

3 tablespoons all-purpose flour

Micro basil, for garnish

**1.** Pile the flour on a clean, dry surface and make a well in the center, like a volcano. Put the eggs and egg yolks into the well. Add 1 tablespoon of the olive oil and a pinch of salt. Using a fork, slowly stir the eggs to break up the yolks, scraping gently along the sides and pulling flour into the well. Continue stirring until most of the flour has been incorporated, and then use your hands to knead the mixture into a smooth dough. If the dough is dry and flaky and you can't mix in all of the flour, add warm water, 1 tablespoon at a time, until the dough feels elastic. Cover with plastic wrap or a clean kitchen towel and let rest for at least 20 minutes and up to 1 hour.

**2.** Roll the pasta dough through a pasta machine, gradually making the dough thinner and thinner, until it is as thin as possible. Cut the dough into 3-inch-wide strips. Place the pasta strips on a semolina-floured baking sheet and cover with a kitchen towel.

**3.** Season the beef cheeks with salt and pepper on all sides. Heat the remaining 2 tablespoons of olive oil in a large pan set over medium-high heat. Add the beef cheeks and cook until browned on both sides, about 2 minutes per side. Transfer to a pressure cooker set to the medium-low setting. Add the onion, garlic, anchovy paste, red pepper flakes, and stock. Cover and cook for 45 minutes. Turn the pressure

*(Continued)*

cooker off and let cool with the lid on for about 5 minutes to reduce steam pressure.

**4.** Using tongs, remove the cheeks from the cooking liquid and transfer them to a food processor. Add ¼ cup of the cooking liquid, reserving the remaining liquid. Pulse until the meat is finely chopped but not completely smooth. Transfer the meat to a medium bowl and stir in the Grana Padano.

**5.** In a large pan, melt the butter over medium heat. Whisk in the flour. While whisking continuously, slowly pour in 2 cups of the beef cooking liquid. Cook, whisking often, until thickened, 1 to 2 minutes. Keep warm.

**6.** To shape the agnolotti, spread the pasta sheets out on a surface dusted with semolina. Spoon 2 teaspoons of the filling 1 to 2 inches apart from one another down the center of each pasta sheet. Brush the edges and spaces in between the filling with the remaining egg wash. Fold the bottom third of the dough up toward the center of the filling and fold down the top third of the dough, overlapping the dough slightly. Using your fingers, gently press out the air between the filling and the pasta. Use a fluted pasta cutter or a small knife to cut between the portions of filling, creating individual agnolotti.

**7.** Bring a large pot of salted water to a boil. Add the agnolotti and cook until al dente, 2 to 3 minutes. Using a slotted spoon, transfer the cooked agnolotti directly to the pan of sauce and toss to coat.

**8.** To serve, place 5 agnolotti in the center of each of four plates. Spoon extra pan sauce over them and garnish with micro basil and grated Grana Padano.

When judge Joe Bastianich tasted this pasta dish, he told Tommy he was mostly looking for the correct ratio of pasta to filling: two-thirds pasta to one-third filling. After taking a bite, he paused for a moment that probably felt like an eternity to Tommy, and then said, "Wow!" Tommy had achieved not only the ideal ratio but also a perfectly seasoned, flavorful pumpkin filling. These ravioli are really delicious served with creamy alfredo sauce, although they would also be fantastic with Sage-Butter Sauce (page 145).

CONTESTANT:
Tommy
—
SEASON 1

# PUMPKIN RAVIOLI
## with CREAMY ALFREDO SAUCE  serves 4

**Pumpkin Ravioli**
Fresh Pasta Dough (page 140)
All-purpose flour, for rolling
Semolina, for dusting
1 cup canned pure pumpkin purée
1 cup ricotta cheese
¼ cup grated Parmesan cheese

2 large eggs
¼ teaspoon freshly grated nutmeg
¼ teaspoon freshly ground black pepper
Kosher salt

**Sauce**
½ cup (1 stick) unsalted butter
1 shallot, minced
1 garlic clove, minced
1½ teaspoons all-purpose flour
1 cup heavy cream
½ cup grated Parmesan cheese
Kosher salt and freshly ground black pepper

**1.** Make the pumpkin ravioli: Using a pasta roller or a rolling pin, roll the dough out to ¹⁄₃₂ inch thick, adding flour as needed to prevent sticking. Use a round cookie cutter or small glass to punch out 2- to 3-inch circles. Place them on a baking sheet dusted with semolina flour and cover with a clean kitchen towel while you prepare the filling.

**2.** In a bowl, combine the pumpkin, ricotta, Parmesan, 1 of the eggs, the nutmeg, pepper, and ½ teaspoon salt.

**3.** Make an egg wash by cracking the remaining egg into a small bowl and beating with a fork.

**4.** Spoon about 1 teaspoon of pumpkin filling into the center of each dough circle, brush the edges with egg wash, and place another dough circle on top. Firmly press the dough circles together, pinching to form a tight seal. Cover the filled ravioli while you assemble the rest of the ravioli.

**5.** Make the sauce: In a large pan, melt the butter over medium heat. Add the shallot and garlic and cook, stirring, until the shallot is translucent, about 3 minutes. Whisk in the flour and cook for 1 minute more. Add the cream and Parmesan. Season with salt and pepper. Keep warm.

**6.** Bring a large pot of salted water to a boil. Cook the ravioli until al dente, 4 minutes. Using a slotted spoon, transfer them directly to the pan of sauce. Toss to evenly coat. Serve immediately, with grated Parmesan sprinkled over the top.

SIDES &
SALADS

If you think you know mashed potatoes like the back of your hand, think again! This recipe has a couple of professional kitchen techniques that make the finished dish turn out perfectly every time. First, the potatoes are placed in a pot with cold water and then heated to a boil, which ensures they cook evenly. Second, a warmed mixture of cream and butter is stirred into the mashed potatoes a little at a time. That way, the cook has control over the consistency of the mashed potatoes and can make them as fluffy or as creamy as he or she likes.

CONTESTANT:
Afnan
—
SEASON 5

# PARMESAN MASHED POTATOES

serves 4 to 6

4 medium russet potatoes
Kosher salt

½ cup heavy cream
4 tablespoons (½ stick) unsalted
    butter

Freshly ground black pepper
Grated Parmesan cheese, for
    serving

**1.** Peel the potatoes, cut them into 1-inch pieces, and place in a large pot. Add enough cold water to cover the potatoes by at least 2 inches. Generously season the water with salt and bring to a boil. Cook until the potatoes are tender all the way through, 15 to 20 minutes. Drain in a colander. Push the potatoes through a ricer into a large bowl. (Alternatively, in a large bowl, mash the potatoes with a potato masher or fork.)

**2.** In a small saucepan, warm the cream and butter over medium heat until the butter has melted completely. Pour the cream-butter mixture, a few tablespoons at a time, into the bowl with the potatoes and stir to incorporate. When the mashed potatoes are your desired consistency, season with salt and pepper. (You may not need to add all the cream-butter mixture.) Sprinkle cheese over the mashed potatoes and serve.

"I feel like *MasterChef Junior* is a great show to get people inspired to cook more in their own kitchens. It's inspirational for kids to learn this important life skill, even if you are not planning on becoming a chef." —Alexander

These roasted potatoes make a terrific side dish or accompaniment to all kinds of fish and meat dishes, such as olive oil–poached salmon (see page 72 for the technique) or Pork and Chorizo Sausage with Quick Sauerkraut (page 96). Many *MasterChef Junior* contestants have cooked roasted potatoes, and while some chose to toss the potatoes in olive oil, others went with melted butter instead. We've combined the best of both for this recipe. Butter lends great flavor, and extra-virgin olive oil, with its higher smoking point, helps the potatoes turn golden brown and crisp around the edges.

# ROASTED POTATOES

serves 4

1 pound small red potatoes, quartered or cut into ½-inch-thick slices

2 tablespoons extra-virgin olive oil

2 tablespoons unsalted butter, melted

Kosher salt and freshly ground black pepper

**1.** Preheat the oven to 400°F.

**2.** In a large bowl, toss the potatoes with the olive oil and butter. Season generously with salt and pepper.

**3.** Spread the potatoes out on a rimmed baking sheet or roasting pan. Roast until golden brown and tender, 15 to 20 minutes. Remove from the oven and serve.

Addison's potato salad is a classic accompaniment to barbecue. It tastes creamy from the mayonnaise in the dressing and also a little tangy from the cider vinegar. Try using fingerling potatoes that are many different colors—red, yellow, and purple! Addison served it alongside the Cola-Braised Pork Ribs with Cola Barbecue Sauce (page 103) and Summer Strawberry Salad (page 179), but it's versatile and delicious with lots of things.

CONTESTANT:
Addison
—
SEASON 4

# POTATO SALAD

serves 4

Kosher salt
1 pound fingerling potatoes
1 pound small Red Bliss potatoes

2 tablespoons Dijon mustard
½ cup mayonnaise
2 tablespoons cider vinegar

3 tablespoons chopped fresh chives
Freshly ground black pepper

**1.** Bring a large pot of salted water to a boil. Add all the potatoes and cook until tender, 15 to 20 minutes. Drain and let cool slightly.

**2.** In a large bowl, whisk together the mustard, mayonnaise, vinegar, and chives.

**3.** Cut the potatoes into bite-size pieces and place them in the bowl of dressing. Toss gently to coat the potatoes evenly. Season with salt and pepper and serve.

This quick and easy side dish goes well with any kind of roasted meat. It's a little bit sweet from brown sugar, and also a little bit spicy from a dash of Cajun seasoning mix. Give it a try this year at your family's Thanksgiving!

# SWEET POTATO PURÉE

serves 4

Kosher salt
4 sweet potatoes, peeled and
    diced

¼ cup packed dark brown sugar
4 tablespoons (½ stick) unsalted
    butter, cut into small pieces

¾ cup heavy cream
Cajun seasoning mix
Freshly ground black pepper

**1.** Bring a large pot of salted water to a boil. Add the sweet potatoes and boil until tender, 10 to 15 minutes. Drain.

**2.** In a large bowl, mash the sweet potatoes using a potato masher or a ricer. Stir in the brown sugar, butter, and cream. Season with Cajun seasoning, salt, and pepper and serve.

The balsamic vinegar glaze on these carrots highlights their natural earthy sweetness. For the best-looking final dish, seek out slender rainbow carrots in beautiful orange, yellow, and purple hues. You could also try using a combination of root vegetables such as turnips, parsnips, and rutabaga. They'll need more time to cook until they're tender, so make sure to boil them until nearly done before finishing cooking in the glaze.

CONTESTANT:
Afnan
—
SEASON 5

# BALSAMIC-GLAZED CARROTS

serves 4

Kosher salt
1 bunch multicolored carrots
2 tablespoons extra-virgin olive oil

Freshly ground black pepper
1 tablespoon balsamic vinegar
½ cup chicken stock

1 tablespoon unsalted butter

**1.** Bring a medium pot of salted water to a boil. Prepare a bowl of ice water. Peel the carrots and trim and discard the tops. Add the carrots to the pot and cook until nearly tender, 2 minutes. Transfer to the bowl of ice water and let cool. Drain the carrots and pat dry with a clean kitchen towel.

**2.** In a large pan, heat the olive oil over medium heat. Add the carrots and season them with salt and pepper. Add the vinegar, shaking the pan to turn the carrots and coat with the vinegar. Add the stock and butter and cook until the liquid reduces to a glaze and the carrots are tender, 5 to 7 minutes. Serve hot.

In the finale episode of Season 3, Nathan presented a creative two-part dish. On one side of the plate, he served this warm roasted baby fennel gratin, which is topped with a cheesy bread crumb crust and thinly sliced French ham. On the other side was a raw Shaved Fennel Salad (page 164). By pairing roasted fennel with raw fennel, Nathan highlighted the nuanced flavor of a single vegetable. What other vegetables could you cook two ways? Try bell pepper or carrot!

CONTESTANT:
Nathan
—
SEASON 3
FINALE!

# ROASTED BABY FENNEL GRATIN

serves 4

2 cups heavy cream
1 cup fennel fronds
1 tablespoon fennel seeds, toasted (see Tip, page 57)

Kosher salt and freshly ground black pepper
1 cup chopped baby fennel
½ cup grated Gruyère cheese

½ cup bread crumbs
1 teaspoon fennel pollen (see Tip)
¼ pound French ham, very thinly sliced

**1.** Preheat the oven to 375°F.

**2.** In a small saucepan, combine the cream, fennel fronds, and fennel seeds and bring to a simmer over medium-high heat. Remove the pan from the heat, cover, and let steep for 20 minutes. Strain through a fine-mesh sieve, discard the solids, and season with salt and pepper.

**3.** Arrange the chopped fennel in four small gratin dishes. Divide the infused cream among the dishes. Bake until the fennel is soft and about half the cream has been absorbed, 15 to 20 minutes.

**4.** In a small bowl, combine the Gruyère, bread crumbs, and fennel pollen. Sprinkle the bread crumb mixture over the fennel gratin and bake until the bread crumbs are golden, 10 minutes. Remove from the oven and scatter the ham over the tops. Let cool slightly and serve.

TIP Fennel pollen is exactly what it sounds like—pollen from a fennel plant! It has the same licorice flavor as fennel, but it's also citrusy and sweet. A little goes a long way. Buy it at specialty spice shops or online.

Here's the second part of Nathan's finale dish from Season 3. Serve it alongside the Roasted Baby Fennel Gratin (page 163) as he did, or just serve it by itself. It's terrific with roasted meat like Roast Beef Tenderloin with Root Vegetable Hash (page 109) or Venison Tenderloin with Braised Cabbage and Parsnip Purée (page 127).

CONTESTANT:
Nathan
—
SEASON 3
FINALE!

# SHAVED FENNEL SALAD

serves 4

3 tablespoons olive oil
1 tablespoon champagne vinegar
1 fennel bulb, very thinly sliced

2 tablespoons chopped fennel fronds
½ grapefruit, segmented and chopped

Kosher salt and freshly ground black pepper

**1.** In a large bowl, whisk together the olive oil and vinegar.

**2.** Add the sliced fennel, fennel fronds, and grapefruit and toss to coat. Season with salt and pepper and serve.

Despite its name, broccoli rabe isn't related to broccoli. Its closest relative is actually the turnip! The leafy green vegetable does indeed resemble turnip tops, and its flavor is much closer to that of a turnip, earthy and a little bitter. Boiling broccoli rabe softens the bitter edge, and a generous splash of olive oil gives this purée a velvety smoothness. Try serving a spoonful of it under a fillet of fish cooked any way (see page 72). It would also be fantastic with Salmon en Croute with Minted Peas and Hollandaise (page 52).

CONTESTANT:
Logan
—
SEASON 2

# BROCCOLI RABE PURÉE

serves 4

Kosher salt
1 bunch broccoli rabe

2 tablespoons extra-virgin olive oil

Freshly ground black pepper

**1.** Bring a large pot of salted water to a boil. Add the broccoli rabe and cook until just tender, 3 to 4 minutes.

**2.** Transfer the broccoli rabe to a blender, reserving the cooking liquid. Add the olive oil and blend on high until completely smooth. If the purée is too thick, add some cooking liquid, 1 tablespoon at a time, until the purée is your desired texture. Season with salt and pepper. Serve.

Faced with a Mystery Box Challenge of cooking with "yucky" ingredients, Sarah made this Brussels sprout stir-fry and bravely served it alongside Fried Sardines (page 29). The judges all agreed it was the best dish of the night, complimenting Sarah on her technique for perfectly cooked Brussels sprouts and pronouncing her the winner. If you love the heat of red pepper flakes, feel free to add more!

CONTESTANT:
*Sarah*
—
SEASON 1

# BRUSSELS SPROUT STIR-FRY

serves 4

1 tablespoon grapeseed oil

3 cups Brussels sprouts, trimmed and halved, or quartered, if large

Kosher salt and freshly ground black pepper

½ onion, thinly sliced

½ cup kalamata olives, pitted and chopped

¼ teaspoon crushed red pepper flakes

¼ teaspoon cayenne

½ cup very thinly sliced fennel

2 tablespoons fresh lemon juice

**1.** In a large pan, heat the grapeseed oil over medium-high heat. Add the Brussels sprouts and season lightly with salt and black pepper. Cook, stirring occasionally, until caramelized and tender, about 4 minutes. Add the onion, olives, red pepper flakes, and cayenne and cook until the onion softens, 1 to 2 minutes. Stir in the fennel and cook just until warmed through.

**2.** Remove the pan from the heat, add the lemon juice, and season with more salt and black pepper. Serve hot.

Given the unfortunate reputation broccoli has as the vegetable all kids dislike, it's a bit ironic how many *MasterChef Junior* contestants choose to cook Broccolini. This recipe makes an appearance in Alexander and Troy's Beef Wellington, in Jack's Broiled Salmon with Coconut Sauce and Avocado Purée (page 50), and in many other dishes on the show. Even though it looks like it, Broccolini is not baby broccoli; they're just close relatives. Broccolini tastes a little sweeter.

# SAUTÉED BROCCOLINI

serves 4

1 pound Broccolini, tough bottoms trimmed
2 tablespoons extra-virgin olive oil

1 shallot, minced
2 garlic cloves, minced
2 teaspoons crushed red pepper flakes

Kosher salt
2 tablespoons unsalted butter

**1.** In a large bowl, combine the Broccolini, olive oil, shallot, garlic, and red pepper flakes. Season with salt and toss to coat evenly.

**2.** In a large sauté pan, melt the butter over medium-high heat. Add the Broccolini and cook, flipping once or twice, until tender, 4 to 6 minutes. Serve.

Tae-Ho masterfully cooked this lemon risotto as a part of the Seared Scallops with Jalapeño-Poblano Salsa (page 75). He used it as a base for the other parts of the dish, but it's also really delicious on its own. To make a perfect risotto, make sure to toast the rice in the pan with the shallot and onion before adding warm chicken stock, one ladleful at a time. Your arm might feel like it is going to fall off from the constant stirring, but it's worth the effort and the wait, and absolutely necessary to create a proper creamy texture!

CONTESTANT:
Tae-Ho
—
SEASON 4

# LEMON RISOTTO

serves 4

4 to 6 cups chicken stock
3 tablespoons extra-virgin olive oil
1 shallot, finely chopped

½ small white onion, finely chopped
1½ cups Arborio rice
1 teaspoon rice vinegar
Zest of 1 lemon

Juice of ½ lemon
2 tablespoons heavy cream
¼ cup grated Parmesan cheese
Kosher salt

**1.** Pour the stock into a saucepan and bring to a low simmer. Keep warm.

**2.** In a large skillet or pot, heat the olive oil over medium heat. Add the shallot and onion and cook, stirring occasionally, until translucent, about 5 minutes. Add the rice and cook, stirring, until toasted, 2 to 3 minutes. Stir in the vinegar. Ladle about ½ cup of the warm stock into the rice and stir continuously until absorbed, about 2 minutes. Continue adding the stock in ladlefuls, stirring until the rice has absorbed all the liquid, before adding the next ladleful of stock. (You may not need to add all the stock.) When the rice is tender and the risotto has a creamy texture, remove the pan from the heat and stir in the lemon zest, lemon juice, cream, and Parmesan. Season with salt. Serve.

Most succotash recipes call for cooking corn directly in a pan on the stove, but in this recipe the corn cooks first on a hot grill, with the husk still surrounding the cob. The husk chars while the corn kernels within cook gently and take on some smoky flavor. You don't have to worry about husking the corn until after it's grilled—easier to prepare, and more delicious in the end! If they're in season, use colorful heirloom tomatoes for the best-looking succotash.

# GRILLED CORN SUCCOTASH

serves 6

6 ears corn, husks on
3 tablespoons grapeseed oil
½ pound Spanish (cured) chorizo, diced

1 cup thinly sliced scallions
4 large tomatoes, chopped
½ cup chopped fresh cilantro

¼ cup fresh lime juice
Kosher salt and freshly ground black pepper

**1.** Heat a grill to high or a grill pan over high heat. Grill the corn in their husks, rotating to cook them evenly, until charred, about 10 minutes. Let cool. Remove the husks from the corn and cut the kernels off the cobs.

**2.** In a large pan, heat the grapeseed oil over medium-high heat. Add the chorizo and cook, stirring, until browned, about 5 minutes. Add the scallions and cook, stirring, until wilted, 2 to 3 minutes. Add the corn and cook, stirring, until soft, 3 to 4 minutes. Remove the pan from the heat.

**3.** Stir in the tomatoes, cilantro, and lime juice. Season with salt and pepper. Serve warm.

This vinegary salad is a refreshing and bright side dish. Try serving it alongside pan-seared fish of any kind, slowly cooked meats like Braised Pork Belly with Apple Cider Glaze (page 100), or, as Nate did on the show, with Soy-Marinated Yellowtail with Sautéed Green Beans and Mushrooms (page 70).

# CUCUMBER AND TOMATO SALAD

serves 4

⅔ cup rice vinegar
¼ cup sugar

2 teaspoons kosher salt
2 English cucumbers

2 cups cherry tomatoes, halved

**1.** In a medium bowl, whisk together the vinegar, sugar, and salt. Whisk until the sugar and salt have dissolved.

**2.** Slice the cucumbers lengthwise as thinly as possible, and then cut each slice lengthwise again to create very thin strips. Place the cucumber strips in a large bowl. Add the cherry tomatoes and the dressing. Toss gently to evenly coat and serve.

Simple and delicious, this is a salad to make in the summertime, when ripe tomatoes are bursting with sweetness and cucumbers are juicy and flavorful. For this dish to look its best, choose cherry tomatoes of many different colors. Fresh burrata cheese is a lot like mozzarella, only it's even more creamy. If you've never tried it, this salad would be a delicious first taste and might inspire you to try serving it in many other ways: on toasted bread, alongside grilled vegetables, or in pasta.

# BURRATA SALAD

serves 4

2 pints cherry tomatoes
(preferably mixed colors),
halved or quartered, if large
2 English cucumbers

Zest and juice of 1 lemon
Kosher salt and freshly ground
black pepper

4 (4-ounce) balls burrata cheese
Extra-virgin olive oil

**1.** Place the cherry tomatoes in a large bowl. Quarter the cucumbers lengthwise, then cut crosswise into ½-inch pieces and add to the bowl. Add the lemon zest and juice. Mix well, then season with salt and pepper.

**2.** Just before serving, tear the burrata into bite-size pieces and add them to the bowl. Season the burrata lightly with salt and pepper and a generous drizzle of olive oil. Toss gently. Taste and season with more salt, pepper, and olive oil if needed.

If you've never tried yuzu juice, get ready for something great! Yuzu is a golfball-size citrus fruit native to Central China. It has a sweet and not overly tart flavor, and here it stands in for the lemon juice or vinegar that would usually be in a salad dressing. Fresh yuzu fruits are difficult to come by, but the bottled juice can easily be found in Asian grocery stores. Addison also used a splash of yuzu juice in her Season 4 finale dish, Spot Prawns with Seaweed Salad, Sour Plums, and Togarashi Puffed Rice (page 23).

CONTESTANT:
Sean
—
SEASON 2

# YUZU SALAD

serves 4

6 tablespoons yuzu juice

2 teaspoons sugar

1 teaspoon freshly ground black pepper

½ cup olive oil

Kosher salt

2 cups arugula

2 cups baby spinach, chopped

2 yellow bell peppers, thinly sliced

2 red bell peppers, thinly sliced

**1.** In a small bowl, whisk together the yuzu juice, sugar, and black pepper. While whisking, gradually add the olive oil. Season with salt.

**2.** Place the arugula, baby spinach, yellow bell peppers, and red bell peppers in a large bowl. Pour in the dressing and toss to evenly coat the vegetables. Serve.

Crisp, pale-green slices of unripe papaya and crunchy raw bell pepper come together in this bright salad. The dressing, which is sweetened with molasses, nicely balances the tartness of the papaya. Make this salad to serve with the Scallop and Smoked Trout Fritters with Romesco Sauce (page 15) or any other fried dish that could use a little tangy lift. You may have some dressing left over— don't let it go to waste! Use it to dress your own favorite combinations of fruits and vegetables, taking inspiration from Jasmine's salad.

CONTESTANT:
Jasmine
—
SEASON 5

# GREEN PAPAYA
# AND BELL PEPPER SALAD

serves 4 to 6

Zest of 2 key limes
1 cup fresh key lime juice
2 teaspoons minced garlic
1 tablespoon molasses

1 tablespoon finely grated fresh ginger
2 teaspoons kosher salt
1 teaspoon freshly ground black pepper

2 cups extra-virgin olive oil
1 green (unripe) papaya
1 yellow or red bell pepper, cut into very thin strips

**1.** In a medium bowl, whisk together the lime zest, lime juice, garlic, molasses, ginger, salt, and black pepper. While whisking, gradually add the olive oil in a thin, steady stream.

**2.** Peel and thinly slice the papaya, discarding the seeds and inner membrane, and place in a large serving bowl. Add the bell pepper. Pour in about half the dressing, toss gently, and then add more dressing if needed to coat the papaya and bell pepper. Serve.

While there is fruit in this salad, don't let that fool you—it's not exactly a fruit salad. It is a lettuce salad, with a twist! Addison cut the whole lettuce heads in half, then brushed them with olive oil and grilled them. That's a technique usually reserved for vegetables like zucchini, peppers, and onions, all of which soften over direct heat. Grilling lettuce accomplishes the same goal—but most important, it brings out a subtle natural sweetness. Serve this with any kind of grilled dish, Braised Pork Belly with Apple Cider Glaze (page 100) or Cola-Braised Pork Ribs with Cola Barbecue Sauce (page 103).

CONTESTANT:
Addison
—
SEASON 4

# SUMMER STRAWBERRY SALAD

serves 4

2 heads red-leaf lettuce
½ cup plus 2 tablespoons olive oil
Kosher salt and freshly ground
   black pepper

1 cup strawberries, sliced
1 cup peeled orange segments
¼ cup chopped fresh flat-leaf
   parsley

3 tablespoons balsamic vinegar
1 tablespoon cola

1. Heat a grill to high or a grill pan over high heat.

2. Remove the large outer leaves from the red-leaf lettuce and cut each head in half lengthwise through the bottom stem. Brush the lettuce halves with 2 tablespoons of the olive oil. Grill until lightly charred, flipping once, about 2 minutes per side. Transfer to a plate, season with salt and pepper, and let cool. Cut or tear the lettuce leaves into bite-size pieces and place them in a large bowl. Add the strawberries, orange segments, and parsley.

3. In a small bowl, whisk together the vinegar, cola, and the remaining ½ cup olive oil. Season with salt and pepper. Pour the dressing over the salad and toss gently to coat. Serve immediately.

DESSERTS

These sandwich cookies are filled with whipped ricotta buttercream and brushed with a zesty lemon glaze. If you like sweet and tart flavors together, these are the cookies for you. Feel free to try substituting a different citrus fruit for the lemon—grapefruit, lime, and orange would all be delicious!

CONTESTANT:
*Kaitlyn*
—
SEASON 4

# LEMON COOKIES
## with LEMON GLAZE and RICOTTA BUTTERCREAM
makes 20 sandwich cookies

### Lemon Cookies
2½ cups all-purpose flour
1 teaspoon baking powder
1 teaspoon kosher salt
1 cup (2 sticks) unsalted butter, at room temperature
2 cups granulated sugar
2 large eggs
Finely grated zest of 1 lemon
3 tablespoons fresh lemon juice

### Ricotta Buttercream
1 cup (2 sticks) unsalted butter, at room temperature
3 cups confectioners' sugar
1 tablespoon heavy cream
15 ounces whole-milk ricotta cheese
½ vanilla bean

### Lemon Glaze
¼ cup confectioners' sugar
1 tablespoon finely grated lemon zest
3 tablespoons fresh lemon juice

**1.** Make the lemon cookies: Preheat the oven to 400°F. Line two baking sheets with parchment paper.

**2.** In a medium bowl, whisk together the flour, baking powder, and salt.

**3.** In the bowl of a stand mixer fitted with the paddle attachment, beat the butter and granulated sugar on medium-high speed until fluffy, about 3 minutes. Add the eggs one at a time and mix until combined. Add the lemon zest and lemon juice. With the mixer running on low speed, gradually add the flour mixture until it is just incorporated. Transfer the batter to a piping bag and pipe 3-inch circles onto the prepared baking sheets, leaving about 2 inches around each one. Bake until the edges are light golden brown, 12 to 15 minutes. Let the cookies cool completely on the baking sheets.

**4.** Make the ricotta buttercream: In the bowl of a stand mixer fitted with the whisk attachment, beat the butter and confectioners' sugar on high speed until creamy. Add the cream and ricotta. Cut the vanilla bean in half lengthwise and use the dull edge of the knife to scrape the tiny black seeds into the bowl. Mix well.

**5.** Make the lemon glaze: In a small bowl, whisk together the confectioners' sugar, lemon zest, and lemon juice.

**6.** Just before serving, brush the tops of the cookies with the glaze. Spread a heaping tablespoon of buttercream on the flat side of half the cookies and top with the remaining cookies.

Gavin put every single kind of chocolate that was in the *MasterChef Junior* pantry into this layered chocolate cake. He called it the "chocoholic delight." So, if *chocoholic* is a word that you've proudly used to describe yourself, then you'll love this cake! You can garnish with your favorite fresh berry, or even drizzle some raspberry sauce (page 186) over each slice.

CONTESTANT:
Gavin
—
SEASON 1

# CHOCOLATE CAKE
## with WHIPPED CHOCOLATE FROSTING

makes one 9-inch three-layer cake

**Chocolate Cakes**

4 cups all-purpose flour, plus more for the pans

2 cups (4 sticks) unsalted butter, plus more for the pans

1 cup unsweetened cocoa powder

1 teaspoon baking powder

1 teaspoon baking soda

1 teaspoon kosher salt

3 cups granulated sugar

4 large eggs

6 large egg yolks

2 cups buttermilk

1 tablespoon plus 1 teaspoon pure vanilla extract

**Whipped Chocolate Frosting**

6 cups confectioners' sugar

1½ cups unsweetened cocoa powder

1 cup (2 sticks) unsalted butter, at room temperature

8 tablespoons heavy cream

2 teaspoons pure vanilla extract

Fresh raspberries, for garnish
Dark chocolate curls, for garnish
White chocolate curls, for garnish

**1.** Make the chocolate cakes: Preheat the oven to 350°F. Butter and flour three 9-inch cake pans, tapping out the excess flour.

**2.** In a medium bowl, whisk together the flour, cocoa powder, baking powder, baking soda, and salt.

**3.** In the bowl of a stand mixer fitted with the paddle attachment, beat the butter and granulated sugar on medium-high speed until light and fluffy, about 3 minutes. Add the eggs and egg yolks one at a time, beating well after each addition. Beat in about one-third of the flour mixture, followed by half the buttermilk, another one-third of the flour mixture, the remaining buttermilk, and the remaining flour mixture. Add the vanilla and beat until just incorporated. Divide the batter evenly among the prepared pans and smooth the tops.

**4.** Bake for 32 to 35 minutes, until the cakes pull away from the sides of the pans. Let cool in the pans for 10 minutes, then run a butter knife around the edges of the pans and invert the cakes onto a wire rack. Let cool completely.

**5.** Make the whipped chocolate frosting: Sift the confectioners' sugar and cocoa powder into a large bowl.

*(Continued)*

**6.** In the bowl of a stand mixer fitted with the whisk attachment, beat together 2 cups of the sugar-cocoa mixture, the butter, and 2 tablespoons of the cream on medium-high speed until smooth. Add another 2 cups of the sugar-cocoa mixture and another 2 tablespoons of the cream and mix well. Repeat twice more, until all the ingredients are combined and the frosting is fluffy. Mix in the vanilla.

**7.** Place one cake layer on a cake stand or serving plate. Spread some of the frosting on top of the cake. Place a second cake layer on top and spread another layer of the frosting on top. Place the third cake layer on top and frost the top and sides of the cake. Garnish with fresh raspberries and chocolate curls.

Looking at these cakes, you might think they are traditional lava cakes, with a gooey melted-chocolate interior. But there is actually a hidden pinch of cayenne pepper in the cake batter, which gives them a tiny kick of heat. This is an easy recipe to double, or even triple, if you are serving more people.

CONTESTANT:
*Sarah*
—
SEASON 1

# LAVA CAKES
## with WHIPPED CREAM and RASPBERRY SAUCE  serves 4

**Lava Cakes**
½ cup (1 stick) unsalted butter, plus more for the ramekins
Granulated sugar, for the ramekins
6 ounces semisweet chocolate
¼ teaspoon ground cinnamon
Pinch of cayenne
Pinch of freshly grated nutmeg

3 large eggs
3 large egg yolks
¾ teaspoon pure vanilla extract
¼ teaspoon pure almond extract
½ cup all-purpose flour
1¼ cups confectioners' sugar

**Whipped Cream**
¼ cup heavy cream
¼ cup confectioners' sugar
1 teaspoon pure vanilla extract

**Raspberry Sauce**
1 cup fresh raspberries, plus more for garnish
½ cup confectioners' sugar, plus more for garnish

**1.** Make the lava cakes: Preheat the oven to 400°F. Butter the insides of four 6-ounce ramekins and sprinkle with granulated sugar. Tap out the excess sugar.

**2.** Set a heat-safe bowl over a pot of barely simmering water (be sure the bottom of the bowl does not touch the water). Combine the butter, chocolate, cinnamon, cayenne, and nutmeg in the bowl and stir until the chocolate is completely melted and smooth. Remove from the heat.

**3.** In a separate large bowl, whisk together the eggs, egg yolks, vanilla, and almond extract. Gradually add the flour and confectioners' sugar, whisking continuously until fully combined. While whisking, slowly pour in the melted chocolate mixture and whisk to incorporate. Divide the batter evenly among the prepared ramekins and place the ramekins on a rimmed baking sheet.

**4.** Bake for exactly 14 minutes, until the sides of the cake are firm and the center is soft. Remove from the oven and let cool for 5 minutes.

**5.** Meanwhile, whip the cream: In the bowl of a stand mixer fitted with the whisk attachment, beat the cream, confectioners' sugar, and vanilla on medium-high speed until the cream holds stiff peaks, 3 to 4 minutes.

**6.** Make the raspberry sauce: In a food processor, purée the raspberries and confectioners' sugar. Strain through a fine-mesh sieve into a bowl to remove the seeds.

**7.** To serve, run a butter knife around the edges of each ramekin to loosen the cakes. Invert each cake onto a dessert plate. Spoon the whipped cream on each cake and drizzle the raspberry sauce over the top. Dust with confectioners' sugar and garnish with a few fresh raspberries.

These individual pineapple upside-down cakes are topped with a dollop of whipped coconut cream, which might surprise you if you're expecting regular whipped cream! It's a small change, but it makes a big difference and ups the tropical flavors going on in this cake. For additional garnishes, you could drizzle the cakes with a spoonful of store-bought guava purée and top with a piece of dehydrated pineapple.

CONTESTANT:
Jasmine
—
SEASON 5
FINALE!

# PINEAPPLE UPSIDE-DOWN CAKE

serves 4

¾ cup (1½ sticks) unsalted butter, at room temperature
¾ cup packed dark brown sugar
6 sprigs fresh thyme
3 tablespoons dark rum
½ cup heavy cream

¼ small pineapple, peeled and cut into ½-inch-thick wedges
1½ cups all-purpose flour
2 teaspoons baking powder
¼ teaspoon kosher salt
1 cup granulated sugar

2 large eggs
1 teaspoon pure vanilla extract
½ cup pineapple juice
1 (14-ounce) can coconut cream (see Tip, page 190)
½ cup confectioners' sugar

**1.** Melt 6 tablespoons of the butter in a small saucepan set over medium heat. Add the brown sugar and thyme and cook, stirring frequently, until the sugar has dissolved, 5 minutes. Pour half the mixture into four 6-ounce ramekins. Return the pan to medium heat, add 2 tablespoons of the rum and the heavy cream, and stir well. Heat, stirring, for 1 minute. Remove the pan from the heat, let cool, and set aside.

**2.** Preheat the oven to 350°F.

**3.** Arrange the pineapple wedges on top of the brown sugar mixture in the ramekins, overlapping the slices slightly to create a spiral.

**4.** In a medium bowl, whisk together the flour, baking powder, and salt.

**5.** In the bowl of a stand mixer fitted with the paddle attachment, beat the remaining 6 tablespoons butter on medium-high speed until light and fluffy, about 3 minutes. Add the granulated sugar and beat for 2 minutes more. Add the eggs one at a time, beating well after each addition. Beat in the vanilla and the remaining 1 tablespoon rum. Add about half the flour mixture and beat on low speed until just blended. Beat in the pineapple juice, followed by the remaining flour mixture. Spoon the batter into the ramekins over the pineapple layer.

**6.** Bake the cakes on the middle rack of the oven for about 45 minutes, until golden brown and a cake tester inserted into the center comes out clean.

*(Continued)*

**7.** Remove the cakes from the oven, poke a few holes in each cake using a toothpick, and then pour the reserved caramel mixture over the tops. Let the cakes cool in the ramekins for 5 minutes. Run a butter knife around the edge of each ramekin to loosen the cake, and then invert each cake onto a dessert plate.

**8.** In the bowl of a stand mixer fitted with the whisk attachment, beat the coconut cream and confectioners' sugar on medium-high speed until the mixture holds soft peaks, 2 to 3 minutes.

**9.** Garnish each pineapple upside-down cake with a dollop of whipped coconut cream. Serve.

TIP You'll find cans of coconut cream on the same shelf as coconut milk in most grocery stores. They look similar, so make sure you grab the right one! If you can't find it, here's a quick tip: Pop a can of full-fat coconut milk into the fridge for 24 hours, then carefully open the can and skim the cream off the top, leaving the coconut water below!

Judge Joe Bastianich told Sean (and Logan, his partner for the cupcake challenge) that the way a cupcake looks is incredibly important. When he opened the cake box and saw these cupcakes garnished with beautiful caramel swirls, he was impressed. But after taking a bite and discovering a surprise raspberry curd filling in the middle, he was truly amazed. Try garnishing other desserts with these caramel swirls for added flair and elegance.

# CHOCOLATE CUPCAKES

## with RASPBERRY CURD and PASSION FRUIT BUTTERCREAM

makes 24 cupcakes

**Chocolate Cupcakes**
2 cups all-purpose flour
½ cup unsweetened cocoa powder
½ teaspoon baking powder
½ teaspoon baking soda
1 teaspoon kosher salt
1 cup (2 sticks) unsalted butter, at room temperature
1½ cups granulated sugar
2 large eggs
3 large egg yolks
2 teaspoons pure vanilla extract
1 cup buttermilk

**Raspberry Curd**
1 pint fresh raspberries
¾ cup granulated sugar
⅓ cup cornstarch
2 large egg yolks

**Passion Fruit Buttercream**
1½ cups (3 sticks) unsalted butter, at room temperature
3¾ cups confectioners' sugar, sifted
½ teaspoon pure vanilla extract
¼ cup passion fruit purée

**Caramel Swirls**
2 cups granulated sugar
½ teaspoon cream of tartar

24 fresh raspberries, for garnish

**1.** Make the choclate cupcakes: Preheat the oven to 350°F. Line two 12-cup cupcake tins with paper liners.

**2.** In a medium bowl, combine the flour, cocoa powder, baking powder, baking soda, and salt.

**3.** In the bowl of a stand mixer fitted with the paddle attachment, beat the butter and granulated sugar on medium-high speed until light and fluffy, 3 minutes. Add the eggs and egg yolks one at a time, beating well after each addition. Beat in the vanilla. Beat in the buttermilk, followed by the flour mixture. Divide the batter evenly among the prepared cupcake cups, filling each three-quarters full.

**4.** Bake for 15 to 20 minutes, until a toothpick inserted into the center of the largest cupcake comes out clean. Remove the cupcakes from the oven and let cool completely.

*(Continued)*

**5.** Meanwhile, make the raspberry curd: In a small saucepan, combine the raspberries, granulated sugar, and ¼ cup water. Cook over medium heat, stirring, until the raspberries soften, about 5 minutes. Strain through a fine-mesh sieve into a bowl, discarding the seeds, and let cool slightly.

**6.** In a separate bowl, whisk together the cornstarch and egg yolks. Whisk the cornstarch mixture into the strained raspberries. Return the raspberry mixture to the saucepan and cook over low heat, stirring continuously, until thick, about 5 minutes. Let cool completely.

**7.** Make the passion fruit buttercream: In the bowl of a stand mixer fitted with the paddle attachment, beat the butter on medium-high speed until light and creamy, about 2 minutes. Reduce the speed to medium and add the confectioners' sugar about ½ cup at a time, beating well after each addition.

Add the vanilla and passion fruit purée and beat on high speed for 10 seconds, until the frosting is smooth.

**8.** Make the caramel swirls: Line a baking sheet with parchment paper. In a small, heavy-bottomed saucepan, combine the granulated sugar, cream of tartar, and ⅓ cup water. Cook over medium heat, without stirring, until the sugar caramelizes and turns an amber color, 10 to 12 minutes. Remove from the heat and immediately drizzle the caramel onto the prepared baking sheet in 24 small, decorative swirls. Let cool.

**9.** When the cupcakes are completely cool, cut a small hole in the top of each cupcake and fill with raspberry curd. Use a pastry bag with a piping tip or a small spatula to frost the cupcakes. Garnish each one with a fresh raspberry and a caramel swirl.

Addison frosted these rich chocolate cupcakes with a super-decadent chocolate ganache and topped them with toasted marshmallows. When you bite into one, you might be surprised to find that there's gooey melted marshmallow hidden in the middle. We'll leave it up to you to decide if these are even better than s'mores!

# MARSHMALLOW CUPCAKES

makes 18 to 20 cupcakes

1 cup all-purpose flour
¼ cup unsweetened cocoa powder
¼ teaspoon baking powder
¼ teaspoon baking soda
½ teaspoon kosher salt
¾ cup sugar

½ cup (1 stick) plus 5 tablespoons unsalted butter, at room temperature
1 large egg
2 large egg yolks
½ cup buttermilk
1 teaspoon pure vanilla extract
2½ cups mini marshmallows

¼ cup chocolate crispy cereal
2 cups semisweet chocolate chips
¼ cup heavy cream
Blue sanding sugar, for garnish (optional)
Edible flowers, for garnish (optional)

**1.** Preheat the oven to 350°F. Line two 12-cup cupcake tins with paper liners.

**2.** In a medium bowl, combine the flour, cocoa powder, baking powder, baking soda, and salt.

**3.** In the bowl of a stand mixer fitted with the paddle attachment, beat the sugar and ½ cup of the butter on medium-high speed until light and fluffy, 3 minutes. Add the egg and egg yolks one at a time, beating well after each addition. Beat in about half the flour mixture, followed by the buttermilk and vanilla, and then the remaining flour mixture. Divide the batter evenly among the prepared cupcake cups, filling each three-quarters full.

**4.** Bake for about 25 minutes, until a toothpick inserted into the center of the largest cupcake comes

out clean. Remove the pan from the oven and let cool completely.

**5.** While the cupcakes cool, set a heat-safe bowl over a pan of simmering water (be sure the bottom of the bowl does not touch the water). Combine 1½ cups of the marshmallows and 3 tablespoons of the butter in the bowl and heat, stirring, until melted and completely smooth. Stir in the cereal and keep warm over very low heat until ready to serve.

**6.** Set a separate heat-safe bowl over a pan of simmering water (again being sure the bottom of the bowl does not touch the water). Combine the chocolate chips, cream, and remaining 2 tablespoons butter in the bowl and heat, stirring, until melted and smooth. Keep warm over very low heat until ready to use.

**7.** Arrange the remaining 1 cup mini marshmallows in a single layer on a rimmed baking sheet. Using a kitchen torch, toast the marshmallows lightly. Let cool completely.

**8.** To assemble the cupcakes, use a 1-inch ring mold to punch out the center of each cupcake (but not all the way through); reserve the punched-out piece. Fill the cavities with the marshmallow-cereal mixture. Place the reserved cupcake piece on top, pressing it back into place. Spread chocolate ganache frosting across the top of each cupcake and top with toasted marshmallows. Garnish with blue sanding sugar and edible flowers, if desired.

Light and very moist, these cupcakes have a zesty lemon flavor and a pronounced basil theme running through them—in the cupcake batter, as a garnish on top of the frosting, and also in the form of basil "dust," which is Logan's clever name for a mixture of finely ground basil and granulated sugar.

CONTESTANT:
Logan
—
SEASON 2

# LEMON-BASIL CUPCAKES
## with LEMON FROSTING and BASIL DUST  makes 24 cupcakes

**Lemon-Basil Cupcakes**
2½ cups all-purpose flour
½ teaspoon baking powder
½ teaspoon baking soda
1 teaspoon kosher salt
1 cup (2 sticks) unsalted butter, at room temperature
1½ cups granulated sugar
2 large eggs
3 large egg yolks

2 teaspoons pure vanilla extract
2 tablespoons finely grated lemon zest
12 basil leaves, finely chopped
1 cup buttermilk

**Lemon Frosting and Basil Dust**
1½ cups (3 sticks) unsalted butter, at room temperature
3¾ cups confectioners' sugar, sifted
½ teaspoon pure vanilla extract
Juice of 1 lemon
12 large basil leaves
1 cup granulated sugar
24 small whole fresh basil leaves, for garnish

**1.** Make the cupcakes: Preheat the oven to 350°F. Line two 12-cup cupcake tins with paper liners.

**2.** In a medium bowl, combine the flour, baking powder, baking soda, and salt.

**3.** In the bowl of a stand mixer fitted with the paddle attachment, beat the butter and granulated sugar on medium-high speed until light and fluffy, 3 minutes. Add the eggs and egg yolks one at a time, beating well after each addition. Beat in the vanilla, lemon zest, and basil. Beat in the buttermilk, followed by the flour mixture. Divide the batter evenly among the prepared cupcake cups, filling each three-quarters full.

**4.** Bake for 15 to 20 minutes, until a toothpick inserted into the center of the largest cupcake comes out clean. Remove the cupcakes from the oven and let cool completely.

**5.** Meanwhile, make the lemon frosting and basil dust: In the bowl of a stand mixer fitted with the paddle attachment, beat the butter on medium-high speed until light and creamy, about 2 minutes. Reduce the speed to medium and add the confectioners' sugar about ½ cup at a time, beating well after each addition. Add the vanilla and lemon juice and beat on high speed for 10 seconds, until the frosting is smooth.

**6.** In a mini food processor or spice grinder, blend the large basil leaves and granulated sugar until the basil is very finely chopped.

**7.** When the cupcakes are completely cool, use a pastry bag with a piping tip or a small spatula to frost each cupcake. Sprinkle the cupcakes with basil dust and garnish each one with a small whole basil leaf.

"This is a home run," judge Graham Elliot said after taking a bite of one of these whoopie pies. There's an amazing contrast between the rich chocolate cake and the fluffy raspberry marshmallow filling. Plus, they are super fun to eat! If you'd like to try flavoring the marshmallow with a different fruit, any fresh berry would be wonderful and could be prepared the same way as the raspberries.

# RASPBERRY MARSHMALLOW WHOOPIE PIES

makes 8 whoopie pies

3 cups all-purpose flour

1 cup unsweetened cocoa powder

2 teaspoons baking soda

½ teaspoon kosher salt

½ cup (1 stick) unsalted butter, at room temperature

1½ cups granulated sugar

2 large eggs

¼ cup vegetable oil

1½ teaspoons pure vanilla extract

1½ cups whole milk

1½ cups mini marshmallows

¼ cup heavy cream

1 pint raspberries, plus 8 for garnish

¾ cup vegetable shortening

1 cup confectioners' sugar, plus more for garnish

**1.** Preheat the oven to 350°F. Line two baking sheets with parchment paper.

**2.** In a medium bowl, whisk together the flour, cocoa powder, baking soda, and salt.

**3.** In the bowl of a stand mixer fitted with the paddle attachment, beat the butter and granulated sugar on medium speed until pale and fluffy, about 3 minutes. Beat in the eggs, vegetable oil, and vanilla. With the mixer running on low speed, beat in about half the flour mixture, followed by half the milk. Then beat in the remaining flour mixture and remaining milk. Spoon about half of the batter into 4 even portions onto each of the prepared baking sheets, leaving about 2 inches around each mound of batter.

**4.** Bake for 8 to 10 minutes, until the tops spring back when lightly pressed. Let the cakes cool completely on the baking sheets. Repeat with the remaining batter to bake 16 cakes total.

**5.** In a small saucepan, melt the marshmallows with the cream over medium heat, stirring continuously. Let cool.

**6.** In a separate small saucepan, bring the raspberries and 1 teaspoon water to a simmer over medium-low heat and cook, stirring occasionally, until the raspberries fall apart, 7 minutes. Strain through a fine-mesh sieve into a bowl, discarding the seeds. Let cool.

**7.** In the bowl of the stand mixer fitted with the paddle attachment, beat the shortening and confectioners' sugar on medium-high speed until fluffy, about 3 minutes. Beat in the cooled marshmallow cream and the cooled raspberry mixture.

**8.** To serve, spoon some of the filling onto the flat side of 8 cakes. Top with the other cakes to form whoopie pies. Dust the whoopie pies with confectioners' sugar and garnish each one with a fresh raspberry.

Traditional Neapolitan cannoli are shaped like cylinders, with open ends where the filling pokes out. But Alexander chose to deconstruct cannoli, creating a layered stack of crispy fried dough rounds and smooth ricotta filling. On the side, he served a blackberry compote, which both looks and tastes fantastic. Impressed with Alexander's ingenuity, judge Gordon Ramsay called this dish "bloody phenomenal." Just goes to show that there'll always be ways to reconfigure a classic dish and turn it into something new!

CONTESTANT:
Alexander
—
SEASON 1
FINALE!

# NEAPOLITAN CANNOLI

serves 8

**Cannoli Shells**
2 cups all-purpose flour, plus more for rolling
5 tablespoons granulated sugar
¼ teaspoon kosher salt
1 tablespoon plus 2 teaspoons unsalted butter, cut into small pieces
½ cup dry white wine
1 large egg yolk

4 cups canola oil
3 tablespoons ground cinnamon

**Filling**
2 cups whole-milk ricotta cheese
¾ cup confectioners' sugar
1 teaspoon ground cinnamon
¼ teaspoon ground allspice
¼ cup heavy cream
¼ cup chocolate chips

Zest of 1 lemon

**Blackberry Compote**
1 tablespoon unsalted butter
2 cups blackberries, rinsed
¼ cup granulated sugar

Confectioners' sugar, for dusting
Blackberries, for garnish
Fresh mint leaves, for garnish

1. Make the cannoli shells: In a medium bowl, sift together the flour, 1 tablespoon of the granulated sugar, and salt. Using your fingers, work the butter into the flour mixture until the dough resembles coarse sand. Add the wine and egg yolk and mix until a smooth dough forms. Shape the dough into a disk, wrap in plastic, and refrigerate while you prepare the filling.

2. Make the filling: In a medium bowl, whisk the ricotta until smooth. Whisk in the confectioners' sugar, cinnamon, and allspice.

3. In the bowl of a stand mixer fitted with the whisk attachment, beat the cream on medium-high speed until it holds stiff peaks, 3 to 4 minutes. Using a rubber spatula, gently fold the cream into the ricotta mixture. Stir in the chocolate chips and lemon zest. Cover and refrigerate for 30 minutes to 1 hour.

4. Make the blackberry compote: In a medium saucepan, melt the butter over high heat. Add the berries and cook, stirring, for 2 minutes. Stir in the sugar until it has dissolved, about 2 minutes. Remove the pan from the heat and let cool.

5. Meanwhile, in a heavy-bottomed pot, heat the canola oil to 360°F. On a floured surface, roll out the dough to ⅛ inch thick. Using the rim of a glass with a 3- to 4-inch diameter, cut out 24 circles, gathering

*(Continued)*

the scraps of dough and rerolling if needed. Working in batches, carefully add the dough circles to the hot oil and fry until golden brown and crisp, 3 to 4 minutes. Transfer to a wire rack, let cool slightly, and then sprinkle with the cinnamon and the remaining 4 tablespoons granulated sugar. Repeat to fry the remaining dough circles.

**6.** Just before serving, transfer the filling to a pastry bag and pipe it across 8 of the fried shells. Gently place a second fried shell on top of each, pipe more filling, and then top with a third fried shell. Dust with confectioners' sugar and garnish with blackberries and mint. Serve the compote on the side.

---

## ALEXANDER'S LOVE OF PASTRY

When that first batch of twenty-four young home cooks walked into the *MasterChef Junior* kitchen for the opening season, everyone was hopeful and excited to find out what kinds of great dishes they'd cook. During that premiere episode, Alexander, who would become the first-ever MasterChef Junior, gave the judges a taste of what was to come with his Pistachio Macarons with Vanilla Caramel Filling (page 229). Later on in Season 1, for the dessert course of the finale episode, he bookended his time on the show by making another impressive pastry, Neapolitan Cannoli (page 201). These delicate European pastries, coming from the hands of such a sweet, talented young man, wowed America and cemented Alexander in the minds of our audience as the young baker from New York with dreams of cooking in professional kitchens. Baking throughout the competition was never a question for him, because, as he says, "I love pastry. It's what I started out doing." At a very young age, Alexander began getting his hands dirty—literally!—baking with his mom and then later cooking with his dad.

His love for pastry has led him to summer jobs in fine-dining establishments. He cooked first at Dominique Ansel Bakery, where he actually worked overnight, constructing all the pastries that are displayed in the morning. More recently, he had a summer job at the French-American restaurant The Dutch, working with Chef Jason Hua. Alexander was able to cook in many different stations of the kitchen, working his way up from preparing cold appetizers to cooking hot entrées. Even though these days Alexander clearly excels at cooking all types of food, America will always remember him fondly as a young pastry protégé.

---

You'll need to plan ahead to make this creamy custard pie. The filling needs an hour or two to chill in the refrigerator, and the fully assembled pie also requires some time to set. All that time will be worth it, though, when you serve a gorgeous slice and taste the sweet-tart flavor of the key lime filling combined with the richness of the coconut whipped cream topping. Feel free to try substituting the key limes with a different citrus fruit, such as lemon or blood orange. You could also garnish the whipped cream topping with fresh raspberries and finely grated citrus zest, if you like.

CONTESTANT:
Levi
—
SEASON 2

# KEY LIME PIE
## with COCONUT WHIPPED CREAM   makes one 9-inch pie

### Piecrust
2½ cups all-purpose flour, plus more for rolling

½ cup (1 stick) unsalted butter, chilled and cubed

¼ cup shortening

Kosher salt

1 large egg

3 tablespoons sour cream

¼ cup cold water

### Key Lime Filling
3 cups plus 2 tablespoons whole milk

1 teaspoon powdered gelatin

4 large egg yolks

½ cup granulated sugar

1 tablespoon pure vanilla extract

⅓ cup cornstarch

2 tablespoons unsalted butter, cut into cubes and chilled

Zest of 2 key limes

2 tablespoons fresh key lime juice

### Coconut Whipped Cream
2½ cups heavy cream

3 tablespoons coconut cream (see Tip, page 190)

¼ cup confectioners' sugar

1 teaspoon pure vanilla extract

Green food coloring (optional)

Key lime zest, for garnish

1 key lime, thinly sliced, for garnish

1. Make the piecrust: In a food processor, combine the flour, butter, shortening, and a pinch of salt. Pulse until the mixture resembles coarse sand.

2. In a small bowl, whisk together the egg, sour cream, and water. Add to the flour mixture and pulse until a dough comes together. Wrap the dough in plastic wrap and refrigerate for at least 30 minutes.

3. Preheat the oven to 400°F.

4. On a lightly floured surface, roll the dough out to an 11-inch circle about ⅛ inch thick. Drape the dough across a 9-inch pie pan. Fold the overhanging edge under itself to make it double thick. Using your fingers, press the edge to create a fluted pattern. Prick the base with a fork. Line the crust with a piece of parchment paper and fill with pie weights, dried beans, or uncooked rice. (For more about blind-baking, see page 208.) Bake on the bottom rack of the oven until the edges are light golden brown, about 20 minutes. Remove the pie weights and parchment and return the crust to the oven to bake until evenly golden, 10 minutes more. Let cool completely.

*(Continued)*

**5.** Make the key lime filling: In a small bowl, combine 2 tablespoons of the milk and the gelatin. Let sit while the gelatin blooms, 5 minutes.

**6.** In a heavy saucepan, heat 2½ cups of the milk over medium heat. As soon as bubbles form around the edges of the pan, remove the pan from the heat.

**7.** In a medium bowl, whisk together the egg yolks, remaining ½ cup milk, the granulated sugar, vanilla, and cornstarch. While whisking, slowly add about 1 ladleful of hot milk to the egg mixture. While whisking continuously, gradually pour the warmed egg mixture into the saucepan. Cook over low heat, whisking continuously, until the custard thickens and coats the back of a spoon, 5 to 7 minutes. Remove the pan from the heat and whisk in the gelatin mixture and the butter. Strain the custard through a fine-mesh sieve into a bowl. Whisk in the lime zest and lime juice. Place a piece of plastic wrap directly on the surface of the custard to prevent a skin from forming and refrigerate until cool, 1 hour.

**8.** Make the coconut whipped cream: In the bowl of a stand mixer fitted with the whisk attachment, beat the heavy cream, coconut cream, confectioners' sugar, and vanilla on medium-high speed until the mixture holds stiff peaks, about 4 minutes. Transfer half the whipped cream to a bowl. If desired, add green food coloring, a few drops at a time, and mix until the whipped cream is your desired shade of green.

**9.** To assemble the pie, spoon the key lime filling into the cooled piecrust and spread evenly. Top with the white coconut whipped cream, spreading it almost all the way to the edges. Transfer the green whipped cream to a pastry bag fitted with the star tip and pipe several decorative mounds, or add dollops of the green whipped cream and spread with the back of a spoon. Garnish with lime zest and sliced lime. Refrigerate for 2 to 3 hours, until set. Serve chilled.

These petite tarts are filled with vanilla pastry cream and topped with a crown of fresh raspberries. A generous brush of apricot glaze makes the fruit glisten beautifully. You can use any kind of fresh fruit in place of the raspberries—try orange segments or a combination of ripe blackberries, strawberries, and blueberries. Nathan served a smooth raspberry sauce on the side and, if you'd like to do the same, see page 186.

CONTESTANT:
*Nathan*
—
SEASON 3

# RASPBERRY VANILLA CREAM TARTS

serves 4

1¼ cups all-purpose flour, plus more for rolling

½ cup (1 stick) unsalted butter, cut into small pieces and chilled

½ cup plus 1 tablespoon sugar

¼ teaspoon kosher salt

¼ cup ice water

4 large egg yolks

¼ cup cornstarch

2 cups whole milk

½ vanilla bean

½ cup apricot preserves

1 pint fresh raspberries

**1.** In a food processor, combine the flour, butter, 1 tablespoon of the sugar, and the salt. Pulse until the mixture resembles coarse sand. Pour in the ice water and pulse until the dough comes together in a ball. Transfer the dough to a flat surface, shape it into a disk, and wrap it in plastic wrap. Refrigerate for 1 hour.

**2.** On a lightly floured work surface, roll out the dough to ⅛ inch thick. Cut the dough into 4 circles, each about 5 inches in diameter. Drape each circle of dough across a 3½-inch tart pan with a removable bottom, pressing the sides and trimming any overhanging edges. Refrigerate for 30 minutes.

**3.** Preheat the oven to 375°F.

**4.** Prick the bottom of the dough crusts with a fork. Line each tart with parchment paper and weigh down the paper with either pie weights or dried beans. (For more about blind-baking, see page 208.) Bake until very lightly golden brown around the edges, about 15 minutes. Remove the weights and parchment and bake until golden, 12 to 15 minutes more. Remove the tart shells from the oven and let cool to room temperature.

**5.** In a medium bowl, whisk together the egg yolks, cornstarch, and remaining ½ cup sugar until pale in color.

**6.** In a heavy-bottomed medium saucepan, bring the milk to a simmer over medium heat. Remove the pan from the heat. Cut the vanilla bean lengthwise and use the dull edge of the knife to scrape the tiny black seeds into the hot milk. While whisking the egg mixture continuously, slowly add about ¼ cup of the hot milk. Pour the warmed egg mixture back

*(Continued)*

into the saucepan and cook, whisking continuously, until thickened, about 5 minutes. Strain through a fine-mesh sieve into a bowl. Cover with plastic wrap, pressing it directly against the surface to prevent a skin from forming. Refrigerate until cold, 1 to 2 hours.

**7.** Combine the apricot preserves and ¼ cup water in a small saucepan and bring to a simmer over medium-low heat. Strain through a fine-mesh sieve into a bowl, discarding the solids, and keep warm.

**8.** To assemble the tarts, spoon a heaping tablespoon of pastry cream into each tart shell and smooth it into an even layer. Arrange the raspberries on top of the pastry cream and brush them with the apricot glaze. Serve immediately or refrigerate, covered, for up to 3 days.

## BLIND-BAKING PIE AND TART CRUSTS

Nathan demonstrated his mastery of a pastry technique called blind-baking, or baking a crust without any filling in it. For a cream pie or tart such as this one, blind-baking the crust is a necessary step, because the cream filling doesn't ever need to cook in the oven. To prevent the dough from puffing up while it bakes, the tart must be lined with parchment paper and then weighed down with dried beans, uncooked rice, or pie weights. Once the crust is nearly set, the weights can be removed to expose the crust and give it a chance to turn golden brown.

You can barely tell by looking at these tart crusts, but they contain finely grated Meyer lemon zest and fresh thyme leaves. The Meyer lemon zest has a subtle yet delightful pine flavor, which partners nicely with the thyme, and together they enhance the already citrusy notes of the Earl Grey–infused pastry cream filling. Such sophisticated flavors for a twelve-year-old! The judges loved the way Nathan included his favorite snack food, pretzels, to give this tart some salty crunch.

CONTESTANT:
Nathan
—
SEASON 3
FINALE!

# EARL GREY TART
## with BLOOD ORANGE COULIS serves 4

1¼ cups all-purpose flour, plus more for rolling

1 cup plus 1 tablespoon sugar

¼ teaspoon kosher salt, plus a pinch

½ cup (1 stick) unsalted butter, cut into small pieces and chilled

1 tablespoon finely grated Meyer lemon zest

1 tablespoon fresh thyme leaves

¼ cup ice water

2 cups whole milk

1 teaspoon pure vanilla extract

5 Earl Grey tea bags

4 large egg yolks

¼ cup plus 1 tablespoon cornstarch

1 cup blood orange juice

4 small pretzels, broken into pieces, for garnish

4 strips candied orange peel, for garnish

**1.** In a food processor, combine the flour, 1 tablespoon of the sugar, the salt, butter, Meyer lemon zest, and thyme. Pulse until the mixture resembles coarse sand. Pour in the ice water and pulse until the dough comes together in a ball. Transfer the dough to a flat surface, shape it into a disk, and wrap in plastic wrap. Refrigerate for 1 hour.

**2.** On a lightly floured work surface, roll out the dough to ⅛ inch thick. Cut the dough into 4 circles, each about 5 inches in diameter. Drape each circle of dough across a 3½-inch tart pan with a removable bottom, pressing the sides and trimming any overhanging edges. Refrigerate for 30 minutes.

**3.** Preheat the oven to 375°F.

**4.** Prick the bottom of the dough crusts with a fork. Line each tart with parchment paper and weigh down the paper with pie weights, dried beans, or uncooked rice. (For more about blind-baking, see page 208.) Bake until very lightly golden brown around the edges, about 15 minutes. Remove the weights and parchment and bake until golden, 12 to 15 minutes more. Remove the tart shells from the oven and let cool to room temperature.

**5.** In a heavy-bottomed medium saucepan, bring the milk to a simmer over medium heat. Remove the pan from the heat and add the vanilla, a pinch of salt, and the Earl Grey tea bags. Cover the pan and let steep for 10 minutes. Remove and discard the tea bags.

**6.** In a medium bowl, whisk together the egg yolks, ¼ cup of the cornstarch, and ½ cup of the sugar until pale in color. While whisking the egg mixture continuously, slowly add about ¼ cup of the infused milk. Pour the warmed egg mixture back into the

*(Continued)*

saucepan and cook, whisking continuously, until thickened, about 5 minutes. Strain through a fine-mesh sieve into a bowl. Cover with plastic wrap, pressing it directly against the surface to prevent a skin from forming. Refrigerate until cold, 1 to 2 hours.

**7.** In a small saucepan, combine the blood orange juice and remaining ½ cup sugar and bring to a simmer over medium heat. Whisk in the remaining 1 tablespoon cornstarch and bring to a simmer once again. Strain through a fine-mesh sieve into a bowl and let cool.

**8.** To assemble the tarts, spoon a heaping tablespoon of Earl Grey cream into each tart shell and smooth it into an even layer. Garnish with the pretzel pieces and candied orange peel. Serve the tarts with the blood orange coulis on the side.

"My advice for anybody who is looking to take their food to the next level is to experiment. At first, don't spend time worrying about what will look prettiest together, or whether or not certain flavor combinations will work. Any mistakes you make will help you learn more." —Nathan

When he made this dish for the finale episode of Season 2, Samuel used dry ice to quickly freeze fresh raspberries. Then he broke up the berries into small pieces and added them as a garnish on top of the panna cotta. It's a cool technique, but you can just use fresh raspberries, too, if you'd like to dress up this dessert.

# PASSION FRUIT GELÉE
## and MAKRUT LIME PANNA COTTA  serves 4

1 cup gingersnap cookies
6 teaspoons powdered gelatin
3 tablespoons cold water
1¼ cups passion fruit purée
  (see Tip)

¾ cup sugar
3½ cups heavy cream
1 cup whole milk
1 vanilla bean

2 makrut lime leaves (see Tip,
  page 63)
Zest of 1 key lime
4 sprigs micro basil, for garnish

1. In a food processor, grind the gingersnap cookies to a powder. Pass the powder through a fine-mesh sieve into a bowl, discarding any large crumbles.

2. In a small bowl, combine 2 teaspoons of the gelatin and 1 tablespoon of the cold water. Let sit until the gelatin blooms, 2 minutes.

3. Meanwhile, in a small saucepan, heat the passion fruit purée over medium heat until it simmers and then remove the pan from the heat. Whisk in ¼ cup of the sugar and the gelatin mixture. Pour the passion fruit mixture into four dessert glasses, filling each one-quarter full. Refrigerate until slightly set, about 1 hour.

4. In a small bowl, combine the remaining 4 teaspoons gelatin and the remaining 2 tablespoons cold water. Let sit until the gelatin blooms, 2 minutes.

5. Meanwhile, in a medium saucepan, bring the cream, milk, and remaining ½ cup sugar to a simmer over medium-high heat. Cut the vanilla bean in half lengthwise and use the dull edge of the knife to scrape the tiny black seeds into the pan. As soon as the cream mixture bubbles, remove the pan from the heat, add the makrut lime leaves and key lime zest, and let steep for 5 minutes. Strain through a fine-mesh sieve into a bowl, discarding the solids. Whisk in the gelatin mixture. Pour the makrut lime panna cotta over the passion fruit gelée, filling the glasses nearly all the way to the top. Refrigerate until set, about 2 hours.

6. Just before serving, dust the top of each panna cotta with the gingersnap powder and garnish with the micro basil.

TIP  You can buy passion fruit purée from specialty foods stores or online. It's often sold frozen because it'll keep for months in the freezer.

Showing off her signature creativity and playfulness, Addison crumbled Pocky Sticks, a beloved Japanese biscuit snack, to make a crunchy bed for silky green tea panna cotta. Judge Christina Tosi absolutely loved this dessert and complimented Addison on the panna cotta's perfect texture.

# GREEN TEA PANNA COTTA
serves 4 to 6

1 teaspoon matcha green tea powder
1½ teaspoons powdered gelatin

1½ cups plus 2 tablespoons heavy cream
1 teaspoon pure vanilla extract

¼ cup sugar
3 packages chocolate-dipped biscuit sticks, such as Pocky Sticks

**1.** In a small bowl, whisk together the matcha and gelatin. Stir in 2 tablespoons of the cream and let sit until the gelatin blooms, 3 to 4 minutes.

**2.** Meanwhile, in a medium saucepan, bring the remaining 1½ cups cream, vanilla, and sugar to a simmer over medium heat. Remove the pan from the heat and whisk in the gelatin mixture. Pour the mixture into four to six small dome-shaped silicone molds or ramekins. Refrigerate until set, 4 to 6 hours. Remove, unmold, and refrigerate until ready to serve.

**3.** Reserve 8 to 12 of the chocolate-dipped biscuit sticks for garnish. Place the remaining sticks in a food processor and pulse until they resemble coarse sand.

**4.** To serve, place a heaping tablespoon of the biscuit crumbles in the center of each plate. Top each with 1 panna cotta. Garnish each with 2 reserved whole chocolate-dipped biscuit sticks.

This stunning layered dessert is made up of three separate parts: a tart raspberry gelée; a smooth, thick raspberry mousse; and a dollop of lime whipped cream. Together they add up to a delicious combination of sweet and creamy in every bite. Instead of raspberries, you could use your favorite fresh berry, and you could also try making the whipped cream with the zest of another citrus fruit.

CONTESTANT:
Andrew
—
SEASON 3

# RASPBERRY MOUSSE, GELÉE,
## and LIME WHIPPED CREAM PARFAIT serves 4

**Raspberry Mousse**
1 pint fresh raspberries
3 large egg yolks
⅔ cup sugar
1¼ cups heavy cream

**Gelée**
1 pint fresh raspberries
¼ cup sugar
1 tablespoon fresh lemon juice
½ teaspoon powdered gelatin

1 tablespoon boiling water

**Lime Whipped Cream**
½ cup heavy cream
1 tablespoon lime zest

1. Make the raspberry mousse: Place the raspberries in a blender and purée until smooth. Strain through a fine-mesh sieve into a bowl and discard the seeds.

2. Set a bowl over a pot of barely simmering water (do not let the bottom of the bowl touch the water). Combine the egg yolks and sugar in the bowl and whisk until the mixture thickens and lightens in color, about 5 minutes. Stir in the raspberry purée and cook, whisking continuously, until the mixture coats the back of a spoon, 3 to 5 minutes. Remove from the heat, set the bowl over another bowl of ice water, and whisk until cooled to room temperature.

3. In the bowl of a stand mixer fitted with the whisk attachment, beat the cream on medium-high speed until it holds stiff peaks, 3 to 4 minutes. Fold the whipped cream into the raspberry mixture. Cover the mousse and refrigerate for at least 20 minutes.

4. Make the gelée: In a medium saucepan, bring the raspberries, sugar, lemon juice, and 3 tablespoons

water to a simmer over medium-high heat. Transfer to a blender and purée until smooth. Strain through a fine-mesh sieve into a bowl and discard the seeds.

5. In a small bowl, stir together the gelatin and 1 tablespoon water. Let sit until the gelatin blooms, 5 minutes. Add the boiling water and stir until the gelatin dissolves. Stir the gelatin into the raspberry purée. Spoon the gelée into the bottom of four dessert glasses. Refrigerate until set, about 20 minutes.

6. Spoon the mousse over the gelée, smoothing the surface, and refrigerate until set, about 20 minutes.

7. Meanwhile, make the lime whipped cream: In the bowl of a stand mixer fitted with the whisk attachment, beat the cream on medium-high speed until it holds soft peaks, 3 to 4 minutes. Fold in the lime zest.

8. Serve each parfait with a spoonful of lime whipped cream on top.

The tropical flavors of coconut milk, mango, and lime come together in this rich, creamy rice pudding topped with a compote that is both tart and sweet at the same time. You could take the tropical theme one step further by garnishing it with other ingredients that evoke island vibes: toasted flaked coconut, fresh papaya and guava, or grilled pineapple (see page 76).

CONTESTANT:
Jenna
—
SEASON 3

# COCONUT RICE PUDDING
## with MANGO COMPOTE  serves 4

**Coconut Rice Pudding**
1 cup jasmine rice
1 (15-ounce) can unsweetened
   coconut milk
1 cup heavy cream

⅓ cup sugar
½ vanilla bean

**Mango Compote**
¼ cup sugar

1 cup chopped fresh mango
Juice of ½ lime
2 teaspoons thinly sliced fresh
   mint

Whole mint leaves for garnish

**1.** Make the coconut rice pudding: Bring 2½ cups water to a boil in a medium saucepan. Add the rice and cook until tender, about 20 minutes. Drain the rice if necessary (all the water may have evaporated) and return the rice to the pot. Stir in the coconut milk, cream, and sugar. Cut the vanilla bean in half lengthwise and use the dull edge of the knife to scrape the tiny black seeds into the pot. Bring to a simmer over medium-low heat and cook until thickened, 10 minutes.

**2.** Meanwhile, make the mango compote: In a small saucepan, combine the sugar, mango, lime juice, and ¼ cup water and bring to a simmer over medium heat. Cook until the mango is soft, 10 minutes. Remove the pan from the heat and stir in the mint.

**3.** To serve, spoon some coconut rice pudding into four glass bowls. Spoon a few tablespoons of the mango compote over the top of each and garnish with mint leaves. (You can choose to serve the rice pudding either hot or chilled.)

Miso is not something you would generally see in a dessert because it has such a savory, salty flavor. But Dara had the confidence to give it a try, plus the creativity to find a way to make it work! The candied ginger is like the cherry on top of an ice cream sundae, a sweet way to finish an already terrific dessert.

CONTESTANT:
Dara
—
SEASON 1

# POACHED PEARS
## with MISO GLAZE and MEYER LEMON CREAM   serves 4

**Poached Pears**
3 cups granulated sugar
Zest and juice of 1 lemon
1 (1-inch) piece fresh ginger, peeled and sliced
1 stalk lemongrass

4 Forelle pears (or other small variety), peeled
2 tablespoons red miso paste

**Meyer Lemon Cream**
1 cup heavy cream
Zest of 1 Meyer lemon
1 tablespoon fresh Meyer lemon juice

1 tablespoon candied ginger, sliced, for garnish
Micro basil, for garnish

1. Make the poached pears: In a medium saucepan, combine the granulated sugar, lemon zest, lemon juice, ginger, and 3 cups water. Trim the root end of the lemongrass stalk and cut off the top 2 inches. Cut the lemongrass in half lengthwise and peel away and discard any tough, papery layers. On a flat surface, use a rolling pin or a meat mallet to smash the lemongrass to release the oils. Place the bruised lemongrass in the saucepan, cutting it again, if needed to fit. Bring the mixture to a simmer over medium-low heat, stirring to dissolve the sugar. Add the pears, cover with a piece of parchment paper cut to fit inside the pot, and cook until the pears are tender, about 20 minutes.

2. Gently transfer the poached pears to a bowl. Discard all but 1 cup of the poaching liquid. Stir in the miso paste until incorporated. Using a fine-mesh sieve, strain the liquid, discarding the solids, and then pour over the poached pears.

3. Make the Meyer lemon cream: In the bowl of a stand mixer fitted with the whisk attachment, beat the cream on medium-high speed until it holds stiff peaks, 3 to 4 minutes. Using a rubber spatula, fold in the Meyer lemon zest and juice.

4. To serve, place 1 poached pear in the center of each of four dessert plates. Spoon some Meyer lemon cream next to the pear and garnish with the candied ginger and micro basil.

Judge Gordon Ramsay looked at this rice pudding with more than a little skepticism at first glance because he grew up eating rice pudding and wasn't so sure the dessert could be modern and delicious. Boy, did Andrew prove him wrong with this creamy, full-flavored, and subtly spiced dessert!

CONTESTANT: Andrew — SEASON 3

# RICE PUDDING
## with FIG-VERJUS REDUCTION   serves 4

**Rice Pudding**
1 cup Arborio rice
3 cups whole milk
4 cinnamon sticks

2 teaspoons pure vanilla extract
1 cup heavy cream
¼ cup sugar

**Fig-Verjus Reduction**
2 cups verjus (see Tip)
1 cup sugar
12 dried white figs
12 dried black figs

4 sprigs fresh thyme, for garnish

**1.** Make the rice pudding: Combine the rice, 2 cups of the milk, 2 of the cinnamon sticks, and 1 teaspoon of the vanilla in a rice cooker with a risotto setting. Select the risotto setting and press start; it takes 20 to 30 minutes to cook. (Alternatively, combine the ingredients in a heavy-bottomed pot and cook over medium heat, stirring continuously, until the rice is tender, about 25 minutes.)

**2.** Meanwhile, in a large saucepan, bring the remaining 1 cup milk, 2 cinnamon sticks, 1 teaspoon vanilla, the cream, and the sugar to a simmer over medium-high heat. Remove from the heat, cover the pan, and let sit for 20 minutes.

**3.** When the rice is finished, remove and discard the cinnamon sticks and transfer the rice directly to the pot with the infused milk. Gently fold until incorporated.

**4.** Make the fig-verjus reduction: In a small saucepan, bring the verjus, sugar, and white and black figs to a simmer over medium-high heat. Cook until the figs soften, 15 minutes. Using a slotted spoon, remove the figs from the liquid and slice into thin rounds. Cook the liquid in the pan until it has reduced by about one-third, 8 to 10 minutes.

**5.** To serve, spoon the rice pudding into four shallow bowls. Spoon the fig-verjus reduction around the edge of each bowl, arrange the sliced figs in the center, and garnish with thyme.

**TIP** Verjus (also known as verjuice) is grape juice made from unripe grapes. It's unlike wine because it's not fermented. It tastes a bit like vinegar, only less acidic. Get it at specialty grocery stores or online.

Sticky toffee pudding might be a familiar dessert, but Alexander's version, with additions of candied fennel and fig purée, tastes extraordinary. Baking the puddings in individual ramekins (instead of one large cake pan) makes them even more special.

# STICKY TOFFEE PUDDING
## with CANDIED FENNEL and FIG PURÉE   serves 7

2 cups heavy cream
2¾ cups packed light brown sugar
¾ cup (1½ sticks) unsalted butter, plus more for the ramekins
6 ounces dates, pitted
1 cup plus 2 tablespoons all-purpose flour

1 teaspoon baking powder
¼ teaspoon baking soda
Kosher salt
1 teaspoon pure vanilla extract
1 large egg
¼ teaspoon finely grated orange zest

½ cup sugar
1 cup thinly sliced fennel
1 cup dried figs, stems removed
Juice of 1 lemon
Whipped cream, for serving

**1.** In a heavy-bottomed saucepan, combine the cream, 2 cups of the brown sugar, and 8 tablespoons of the butter. Cook over medium heat, stirring, until the sugar has dissolved. Let cool to room temperature.

**2.** Preheat the oven to 350°F. Butter the inside of seven 8-ounce ramekins.

**3.** In a small saucepan, combine the dates and ¾ cup water. Cook over medium heat until the dates are soft, about 15 minutes. Transfer the mixture to a blender, purée, and let cool.

**4.** In a small bowl, stir together the flour, baking powder, baking soda, and a pinch of salt.

**5.** In the bowl of a stand mixer fitted with the paddle attachment, beat the remaining ¾ cup brown sugar and remaining 4 tablespoons butter on medium-high speed until light and fluffy, about 3 minutes. Beat in the vanilla, egg, orange zest, and cooled fig purée. Beat in the flour mixture. Divide the batter evenly among the prepared ramekins.

**6.** Bake for about 20 minutes, until the edges pull away from the sides of the ramekins and the puddings are set in the middle. Let the puddings cool slightly before removing them from the ramekins.

**7.** Reduce the oven temperature to 300°F. Line a baking sheet with parchment paper.

**8.** In a small saucepan, combine the sugar and ½ cup water and cook over medium heat, stirring, until the sugar has dissolved. Add the fennel to the syrup, and cook until soft and translucent, about 10 minutes. Using a fork, lift out each slice of fennel and arrange in a single layer on the prepared baking sheet. (Reserve the syrup.) Bake until a little dry but still sticky, 10 minutes.

**9.** Put the dried figs in the reserved syrup and let rehydrate for 5 minutes. Transfer to a food processor and purée until smooth. Stir in the lemon juice.

**10.** To serve, place 1 cake on each of seven dessert plates. Spoon the toffee sauce over the tops. Garnish with candied fennel, fig purée, and whipped cream.

Making soufflé is a real challenge, even for professional chefs! In order to master it, you have to know a few kitchen techniques and skills: First, you must separate the egg yolks from the whites. Then, you warm up the milk and whisk in the cornstarch. From there, you need to either melt chocolate or make a fruit purée. The egg whites must be whisked until they are shiny and firm but not overwhipped. Timing is everything. Before the soufflé challenge on the show, Addison had never tried making a soufflé, and yet she presented this perfect dish to the judges, who all agreed she had nailed it.

# BLACKBERRY SOUFFLÉ
serves 8

1 pint blackberries
2 tablespoons fresh lemon juice
1¼ cups sugar, plus more for the ramekins

3 tablespoons unsalted butter, plus more for the ramekins
2 cups whole milk
1 vanilla bean

¼ cup cornstarch
4 large egg yolks
10 large egg whites
1 teaspoon kosher salt

**1.** In a small saucepan, combine the blackberries, lemon juice, and ½ cup of the sugar. Cook over medium heat, stirring occasionally, until the sugar has dissolved, about 5 minutes. Reduce the heat to medium-low and simmer until the berries soften and collapse, 4 to 5 minutes. Transfer the mixture to a blender and purée until smooth. Strain through a fine-mesh sieve into a bowl, discarding the seeds, and refrigerate until cold.

**2.** In a small saucepan, combine the butter and 1 cup of the milk and heat over medium heat, stirring to melt the butter. Cut the vanilla bean in half lengthwise and use the dull edge of the knife to scrape the tiny black seeds into the pot.

**3.** In a medium bowl, whisk together the remaining 1 cup milk, the cornstarch, and the egg yolks. While whisking the egg mixture continuously, slowly pour

about ¼ cup of the hot milk mixture into the egg mixture. Pour the warmed egg mixture into the pot and cook, whisking continuously, until thickened, about 5 minutes. Strain the mixture through a fine-mesh sieve into a bowl, discarding any solids, and refrigerate until cold.

**4.** Preheat the oven 375°F.

**5.** Use a pastry brush to coat the bottoms and sides of eight 6-ounce ramekins with butter, and then sprinkle with sugar, tapping out any excess.

**6.** In the bowl of a stand mixer fitted with the whisk attachment, beat the egg whites on medium-high speed until frothy, 1 minute. Add the salt and the remaining ¾ cup sugar and beat until the egg whites hold stiff peaks, 3 to 5 minutes.

*(Continued)*

**7.** Measure out 150 grams of the chilled vanilla pastry cream base into a large bowl. Add ⅔ cup of the chilled blackberry coulis and whisk to thoroughly combine. Mix in one-third of the whipped egg whites, and then use a rubber spatula to gently fold in the remaining egg whites. Divide the mixture evenly among the prepared ramekins and smooth the top of each one.

**8.** Bake for 16 to 18 minutes, until the soufflés have risen. Do not open the door as the soufflés bake, otherwise they will deflate. Serve immediately.

## ADDISON'S TIPS FOR MAKING SOUFFLÉ AT HOME

A perfectly risen soufflé, puffy and grand, is an impressive sight to behold. It can seem almost as if there's a bit of magic involved. But, of course, kitchen knowledge and "insider" skills are the real secrets to soufflé.

In one of the final cooking challenges of Season 4, Addison made her first-ever soufflé, choosing to use bold blackberries for a truly beautiful soufflé that wowed the judges. Most people—even professional chefs—would likely have felt a little nervous placing the soufflé in the oven during such an important challenge, but Addison says she felt pretty confident during this challenge because she loves baking so much. "When I am cooking or baking, I don't think too much about what could go wrong," she says. "I just stay focused on what I am doing." She does have one tip for home cooks who are looking to master the soufflé: "The trick is not to overmix the ingredients so you have the right amount of air for the soufflé to be fluffy." And, in the end, "if something doesn't work out," Addison says, "have a sense of humor about it and try it again a different way!"

Pistachio is such a classic flavor for French macarons and a great place to begin if you are just starting out and learning how to make these impressive cookies. One sign of a perfectly baked macaron is the "foot," a little ridge around the base of each cookie. For this version here, finely ground pistachios, with their light green color, add a pleasing color and nutty flavor. Once you have the hang of this recipe, try substituting other finely ground nuts, such as hazelnuts or walnuts, to create your own custom flavor. If you do, be sure to leave out the green food coloring!

CONTESTANT:
Alexander
—
SEASON 1

# PISTACHIO MACARONS

## with VANILLA CARAMEL FILLING *makes 8 macarons*

**Pistachio Macarons**
2 cups confectioners' sugar
½ cup almond flour
1 cup finely ground unsalted pistachios
4 large egg whites, at room temperature

½ teaspoon cream of tartar
½ cup granulated sugar
4 to 6 drops of green food coloring (optional)
Kosher salt

**Vanilla Caramel Filling**
7 ounces condensed milk
1 tablespoon unsalted butter
1 teaspoon pure vanilla extract
Kosher salt
1 vanilla bean
2 tablespoons heavy cream

1. Make the pistachio macarons: Line two baking sheets with parchment paper.

2. Sift the confectioners' sugar, almond flour, and pistachios together into a bowl.

3. In the bowl of a stand mixer fitted with the whisk attachment, beat the egg whites on medium-high speed until foamy, 1 minute. Add the cream of tartar and granulated sugar and beat on medium-high speed until glossy, soft peaks form, 3 to 4 minutes. Using a spatula, fold in about half the almond flour mixture, add the green food coloring (if using) and a pinch of salt, and then fold in the remaining almond flour mixture and mix just until combined. Transfer the batter to a piping bag fitted with a plain round ½-inch tip.

4. Pipe 16 (1½-inch) circles of batter onto the prepared baking sheets, leaving at least 1 inch of space around each circle. Use a wet fingertip to press down any peaks. Tap the baking sheets firmly on a flat surface to release any air bubbles and set aside at room temperature for 30 minutes.

5. Preheat the oven to 325°F.

6. Bake for 15 to 17 minutes, rotating the baking sheets halfway, until the tops of the macarons appear dry. Let the cookies cool completely on the baking sheets.

7. Make the vanilla caramel filling: In a medium saucepan, heat the condensed milk, butter, vanilla extract, and a pinch of salt over medium-high heat.

*(Continued)*

Slice the vanilla bean in half lengthwise and use the dull edge of the knife to scrape the tiny black seeds into the pan. Cook, stirring occasionally, until slightly thickened, 3 minutes. Add the cream, reduce the heat to low, and cook until thick enough to coat the back of a spoon, about 5 minutes. Transfer the mixture to a bowl and let cool.

**8.** To assemble the macarons, spread a layer of filling across the bottom of one pistachio macaron and sandwich another on top. Macarons are best eaten the day they are made.

Nathan nailed it with these macarons that judge Graham Elliot said tasted "like eating a banana-flavored cloud, light and airy." You can make all sorts of delicious-tasting macarons just by changing up the type of flour and filling you use. For instance, in Season 5, Jasmine created piña colada macarons by using almond flour for the cookies and sandwiching them together with a pineapple-coconut filling. Although she was making a French dessert, she really embraced her Caribbean roots with her choice of flavors.

# BANANA AND SALTED CARAMEL MACARONS

makes 12 macarons

**Macarons**
1 cup almond flour
1⅔ cups confectioners' sugar
3 large egg whites
¼ cup granulated sugar

**Filling**
½ cup granulated sugar
¾ teaspoon unsalted butter
1 tablespoon heavy cream
¾ teaspoon flaky salt
1 ripe banana, peeled and puréed

**1.** Make the macarons: Line two baking sheets with parchment paper.

**2.** Sift the almond flour and confectioners' sugar together into a bowl.

**3.** In the bowl of a stand mixer fitted with the whisk attachment, beat the egg whites on medium-high speed until foamy, 1 minute. Gradually add the granulated sugar and beat until glossy, soft peaks form, 3 minutes. Using a spatula, fold in the almond flour mixture. Transfer the batter to a piping bag fitted with a plain round ½-inch tip.

**4.** Pipe 24 (1½-inch) circles of batter onto the prepared cookie sheets, leaving at least 1 inch of space around each circle. Use a wet fingertip to press down any peaks. Tap the baking sheets firmly on a flat surface to release any air bubbles and set aside at room temperature for about 1 hour.

**5.** Preheat the oven to 260°F.

**6.** Bake for about 10 minutes, just until the macarons are set. Do not let them brown. Let cool completely on the baking sheets.

**7.** Make the filling: In a small saucepan, combine the granulated sugar and 1 tablespoon water, and cook over medium-high heat, without stirring, until the sugar melts and caramelizes to an amber color, 10 to 15 minutes. Stir in the butter, cream, and flaky salt. Remove the pan from the heat and let cool slightly, then whisk in the banana purée. Let cool completely.

**8.** To assemble the macarons, spread a layer of filling across the bottom of one cookie and sandwich another cookie on top. Macarons are best eaten the day they are made.

What's more delightful than a warm churro? A warm *chocolate* churro—especially when dipped into toasted marshmallow whipped cream! When Jesse presented these churros to judge Christina Tosi, the first thing that happened was they figured out that they're pretty much neighbors in New York. Then, after Christina took a bite, she decided that they must also be "soul mates" because they both agree on what makes a great dessert.

# CHOCOLATE CHURROS
## with TOASTED MARSHMALLOW WHIPPED CREAM  serves 4 to 6

**Chocolate Churros**
⅔ cup unsalted butter
1¼ cups granulated sugar
1 teaspoon kosher salt
2 cups all-purpose flour

4 large eggs
½ cup mini marshmallows
Vegetable oil, for frying
1 tablespoon ground cinnamon
1 tablespoon unsweetened cocoa
   powder

**Whipped Cream**
1 cup mini marshmallows
1 cup heavy cream
¼ cup confectioners' sugar

**1.** Make the chocolate churros: In a medium saucepan, bring the butter, ¼ cup of the sugar, the salt, and 2 cups water to a simmer over medium heat, stirring until the butter has melted. Using a wooden spoon, stir in the flour. Cook, stirring, until some moisture has evaporated, 2 to 3 minutes. Transfer the dough to the bowl of a stand mixer fitted with the paddle attachment. Beat on low speed for 1 minute, then increase the speed to medium-low and add the eggs one at a time, mixing well after each addition. Reduce the speed to low and add the mini marshmallows.

**2.** Pour at least 2 inches of vegetable oil into a heavy-bottomed pot. Heat over medium-high heat to 375°F.

**3.** In a small bowl, whisk together the cinnamon, cocoa powder, and remaining 1 cup sugar. Transfer to a large plate or shallow dish.

**4.** Transfer the dough to a piping bag fitted with a large star tip. Squeeze about 3 inches of dough from the piping bag over the hot oil, carefully letting the

dough fall into the oil. Repeat to form five 3-inch-long churros. Fry until dark golden brown and cooked through, about 5 minutes. Transfer to a wire rack and let cool. Repeat with the remaining batter.

**5.** While the churros are still hot, roll them in the cinnamon-sugar mixture, shaking off any excess.

**6.** Make the whipped cream: Spread the mini marshmallows in a single layer on a rimmed baking sheet. Use a kitchen torch to toast the marshmallows. (Alternatively, toast them under a broiler.)

**7.** In the bowl of a stand mixer fitted with the paddle attachment, beat the cream and confectioners' sugar on medium-high speed until it holds soft peaks, 3 minutes. Add the toasted marshmallows and whip until the cream holds stiff peaks, 1 to 2 minutes more.

**8.** To serve, place a scoop of the toasted marshmallow whipped cream in the center of each plate. Arrange the chocolate churros around the cream.

In the finale episode of Season 2, Logan blew the judges away with this dessert. The goat cheese mousse seemed a little odd at first, but after taking a bite, judge Graham Elliot praised the dish as "sophisticated and balanced." It's kind of like eating a cheese course at the same time as your dessert! Goat cheese works great because it's creamy and pretty mild tasting. Feel free to try substituting your favorite kind of soft, fresh cheese.

CONTESTANT:
Logan
—
SEASON 2
FINALE!

# MEYER LEMON MADELEINES
## with BASIL–GOAT CHEESE MOUSSE and BERRIES  makes 24 madeleines

**Basil–Goat Cheese Mousse**
6 ounces goat cheese, at room
   temperature
¼ cup confectioners' sugar
3 tablespoons heavy cream

**Berries**
1 cup blackberries
1 cup blueberries
2 tablespoons Meyer lemon juice
¼ cup granulated sugar

**Meyer Lemon Madeleines**
Butter, for the pans
All-purpose flour, for the pans
3 large eggs
2 large egg yolks
¾ cup granulated sugar
1½ cups cake flour, sifted
½ teaspoon baking powder
¼ teaspoon kosher salt
1 teaspoon pure vanilla extract

2 tablespoons Meyer lemon zest
2 tablespoons fresh Meyer lemon
   juice
¾ cup (1½ sticks) unsalted butter,
   melted

Micro basil, for garnish

**1.** Make the basil–goat cheese mousse: In a medium bowl, combine the goat cheese, confectioners' sugar, and heavy cream. Transfer to a piping bag fitted with a plain round tip and refrigerate for 20 minutes.

**2.** Make the berries: In a medium saucepan, bring the blackberries, blueberries, Meyer lemon juice, and granulated sugar to a simmer over medium heat. Cook, stirring often, until the berries collapse, 15 minutes. Let cool.

**3.** Make the Meyer lemon madeleines: Preheat the oven to 375°F. Butter and flour two 12-well madeleine pans.

**4.** In the bowl of a stand mixer fitted with the whisk attachment, beat the eggs, egg yolks, and granulated sugar on medium-high speed until pale and creamy, about 3 minutes. Beat in the cake flour, baking powder, salt, vanilla, Meyer lemon zest, and Meyer lemon juice. Using a rubber spatula, fold in the melted butter. Pour the batter into the prepared madeleine pans.

**5.** Bake for 14 to 17 minutes, until the madeleines spring back when lightly pressed.

**6.** To serve, spoon some berries into the center of each dessert plate. Lean 3 madeleines against the berries on each plate. Pipe a few small mounds of basil–goat cheese mousse around the plate and garnish with the micro basil.

# ACKNOWLEDGMENTS

*MasterChef Junior* would like to thank:

The team at Endemol Shine North America: Thomas Ferguson, Elizabeth M. Lockwood, Kelly Hill, Tamaya Petteway, and Vivi Zigler. Also, our friends on the Marketing Team, Rob Hughes and Ivana Zbozinek, and everyone at the production company who worked behind the scenes.

Our team at Clarkson Potter: Rica Allannic, Doris Cooper, Ian Dingman, Stephanie Huntwork, Ashley Meyer, Kim Tyner, Aaron Wehner, Joyce Wong.

Our talented writer, Maria Zizka, and her agent, Katherine Cowles.

Our excellent photography team: photographer Evan Sung, food stylist Rebecca Jurkevich, and prop stylist Kira Corbin. A special thanks to our cover model, Charlotte Wing-Yi Sweet.

Our entire TV network family and partners at FOX, especially those who helped shepherd this to life:

Melissa Gold, Armando Solares, Kathryn Brown, and Malaika Naulls.

The *MasterChef* judges and production team: Gordon Ramsay, Christina Tosi, Graham Elliot, Joe Bastianich, Robin Ashbrook, Adeline Ramage Rooney, Yasmin Shakleton, the teams at CAA and Milk Bar. We'd also like to thank Chef Sandee Birdsong and Chef Avery Pursell and the talented culinary teams, as well as the fantastic production crews who have worked on the show across the show's seasons.

Most important, to the hundreds of kids who have stepped foot in the *MasterChef Junior* kitchen with big dreams and even bigger hearts. You are what makes this show what it is.

And to the fans, from all of us who work to bring this show to life in all its forms, we thank you! Keep watching and keep cooking!

# INDEX